Catherine Marshall's
Story Bible

Catherine Marshall's
Story Bible

Illustrated by Children

◆ **AVON**
PUBLISHERS OF BARD, CAMELOT, DISCUS AND FLARE BOOKS

Originally published in France under the title: *La Bible illustrée par des enfants* with text by Didier Decoin.

The Crossroad Publishing Company edition contains the following Library of Congress Cataloging in Publication Data:
Marshall, Catherine, 1914- 1983
   Catherine Marshall's Story Bible.
   Adaptation of: La Bible illustrée par des enfants/ racontée par Didier Decoin.
   Summary: Retells thirty-seven stories from the Old and New Testament.
   1. Bible stories, English. [1. Bible stories]
I. Decoin, Didier, 1945-   . Bible illustrée par des enfants. II. Title. III. Title: Story Bible.
BS551.2.M35   220.9'505   82-1361

AVON BOOKS
A division of
The Hearst Corporation
1790 Broadway
New York, New York 10019

English text copyright © 1982 by Catherine Marshall
Original edition copyright © 1980 by Exaequo, Geneva

Published by arrangement with The Crossroad Publishing Company, Inc.
Library of Congress Catalog Card Number: 82-1361
ISBN: 0-380-69961-3

First Avon Printing, April, 1985

AVON TRADEMARK REG. U. S. PAT. OFF. AND IN OTHER COUNTRIES, MARCA REGISTRADA, HECHO EN U.S.A.

Printed in the U.S.A.

10 9 8 7 6 5 4 3 2 1

CONTENTS

Preface   **11**

THE OLD TESTAMENT

Our World Begins   **14**
The First Man and Woman   **22**
One Tricky Snake   **26**
A Jealous Brother   **33**
The Biggest Flood   **35**
A Tower That Touched the Clouds   **40**
The Father Who Obeyed   **45**
Twin Brothers Who Hated Each Other   **50**
The Dreamer Who Saved His People   **56**
A Baby Is Rescued   **65**
"Let My People Go"   **71**
Walk Through the Sea   **78**
God's Thunderclap   **82**
A Shepherd Boy Fights a Giant   **93**
The Wisest Man   **101**
In the Lions' Den   **108**

THE NEW TESTAMENT

The Night Visitor   **118**
A King Is Born   **125**
Following a Wandering Star   **130**
The Missing Boy   **132**
The Voice and the Dove   **134**
The Wedding Party   **138**
The Happiest People   **140**

One Withered Hand 144
Storm at Sea 148
The Healing Touch 149
Why Jesus Loved Children 156
Five Thousand Hungry People 158
Miracle at Bethany 161
Triumphant Ride on a Donkey 167
The Last Supper 170
Betrayed 171
The Strange Trial 178
That Terrible Day! 180
The Empty Tomb 186
Jesus Returns 189
The Gift of New Power 193

PREFACE

One afternoon I walked into my home office to find in the day's mail one of the most enchanting books I had ever seen. Coffee-table size, it had eighty beautiful, four-color reproductions of paintings done entirely by children to illustrate Bible stories. The text was in French and the book had come from Switzerland.

I was being asked to write an English text of the Bible stories for a proposed American edition. Committed to other projects, my first reaction was definitely "No."

But I kept returning to have yet another look at the vivid originality of the children's art work. Curiosity piqued me, then turned into such deep interest that finally I agreed to undertake the English text.

In some ways the writing of these always-exciting, timeless, and priceless stories was less difficult than tracking down the tale behind the book. First, I learned that the illustrations had all been done by children ages six to ten in the art classes of French-born Michèle Kenscoff, for twenty years a teacher in France and in the environs of Geneva.

Yet how had Michèle sparked imaginative work of such excellence in young children?

The day came when I was able to make telephone contact with Michèle Kenscoff's husband at his Swiss office. A future telephone interview was set up. Only, since Michèle did not trust her English, nor I, my French, all my questions would have to be relayed through Pierre Kenscoff.

Out of that three-way conversation the behind-the-scenes of the *Story Bible* emerged . . . Michèle's father is an artist. From girlhood his daughter has had two loves—drawing and painting, and children.

What gave Michèle greatest delight became her profession—the joy of inspiring little folk to draw and paint. Into this teacher's art classes in southwest French-speaking Switzerland eventually would come more than six hundred children from all continents, from Europe and America, from Africa and Asia and Australia.

A Swiss school such as the *École Cantonale* is typical of the melting pot of nationalities that the wider Geneva area has attracted since the time of John Calvin and his international academy with its six separate "faculties." Michèle's students were the sons and daughters of parents who worked for the International Red Cross, the Students' International Union, the International Labour Office, or branches of an astonishing variety of business firms. For since the sixteenth century this section of Switzerland has been a crossroads of cultural activity, as well as a center of both Protestantism and Catholicism.

When I learned that French was used in the classrooms, I asked Pierre if there was any language barrier with children from so many countries.

Over the telephone I could hear Michèle's musical laugh in the background. "No, children can always manage. Their fresh minds don't erect fences as adults do."

At my request, Pierre described his wife . . . Of medium height, Michèle has merry blue eyes and long, auburn-brown hair, sometimes loose around her shoulders, at other times worn in a ponytail. She also is a teacher with a rare sensitivity and patient calmness with children.

The pictures in this beautiful book are the work of many child artists over a fifteen-year period. Sometimes Michèle would relate a Bible story in her own words. Upon occasion, there would be a model for inspiration, but always, the students were allowed to give free rein to their own imaginations. For in the magic land where children gambol, there are no inhibitions. For instance, when Pharaoh's soldiers were painted to resemble knights from the Middle Ages, and the women at Jesus' tomb on Resurrection morning were clothed in European peasant fête costumes, the teacher did not interfere.

Sometimes the children worked at the drawings alone, sometimes in groups of four or five. Their work would then be discussed, compared with others, criticized. But any suggested changes made were always made by the children themselves. No adult has touched the paintings in this book.

With a picture like the jungle one, the teamwork on it often extended over a period of time: nine boys were each allowed to draw an animal of his choice. Democratic group discussion decided to focus on foliage as the background. Each boy, in turn, drew and painted part of the foliage.

The fish took many years to complete. Michèle Kenscoff selected the best drawings, then had her young artists cut them out and glue them on a picture of the sea they had already prepared. This original picture—five feet wide by sixteen feet long—is the work of six classes. Special pens, either one called *Neo-color* or a French *Feutre* (felt) pen, were used for all the vibrant coloring.

What challenged me as I worked on the *Story Bible* is the opportunity it presents to young children to see and hear about God's ways with His children, and about the glorious difference Jesus Christ has made in the lives of so many people. It is for this reason that parents and grandparents, friends and godparents will find this such a valuable gift book. The *Story Bible* will also be a conversation piece around many a coffee table because adults are endlessly intrigued with the fresh originality of children's minds.

And so, I give you, with all-out enthusiasm, the *Story Bible*.

Catherine Marshall

January 6, 1982

THE OLD TESTAMENT

OUR WORLD BEGINS

Genesis 1:1–25

Did you awake this morning with the warm light of the sun shining in an arch of blue sky? Outside your window were the limbs of trees lifting up their arms, swaying gently in the wind? The good earth to wiggle your toes in, soft grass to lie in, fragrant flowers of every color to touch?

It seems strange to think that our earth-home has not always been like that. Long, long ago, there was a time—yes, even before time began—when there was no earth, nor rivers and oceans; no sun or moon or twinkling stars—nothing but darkness and silence and empty space.

Yet even in this vast emptiness there was God, for He has always been there. But God's great heart was lonely. God is made of love. So the love that filled Him wanted to create beauty and longed for fellow creatures with a spirit like His to receive His love.

Now in God there was light and life. Since that was so, all He had to do was to let the light and life flow out in the Words He spoke. Then what He spoke would be created.

First, He set to work filling the vast empty space around Him by stretching the dark sky in all directions, like an artist unrolling his canvas. Then He created water. After that He fashioned the earth.

But the earth still had no form, and everywhere there was darkness. So the Creator-God spoke the Word, "Let there be light."

As if a spark had flown from His lips, the light that was in Him flowed out, and immediately light appeared. Like warm, golden ripples it spread around Him. He found it beautiful, golden, and comforting. Then He gave it the name "Day." The remaining darkness God called "Night."

God created the heavenly lights

On the second day, God divided the waters: the water from above He separated from the waters below.

In between the waters God made the sky out of a wonderful blue: a light blue for the day, a darker blue for the night. "Heaven" is what God called the sky.

On the morning of the third day, God saw down in a far corner of space the earth spinning, a tiny ball covered with mighty oceans of water.

Again God spoke a Word, calling dry land up from the ocean floor. With a roar, mighty waves rolled aside as mountains rose toward the sky. Waters rushed down the cliffs, forming streams, rivers, and bays. At last they settled into the deep bowls of the earth, rocking back and forth from shore to shore in a foaming tide.

Now God stood at the rim of the sea. The rocks felt firm and strong beneath His feet. Far in the distance, the blue sky touched the towering mountains for the first time.

The dry land God called "Earth" and the gathering together of the waters He named "Seas."

Then God spoke to the soil, and plants of every color broke through the ground. Green pine trees covered the hills. Daisies opened their yellow eyes in the meadows. Purple orchids clung to secret, rocky caves in tropical islands. Apples, oranges, cherries, raspberries, blueberries—every kind of fruit popped from the branches of trees and bushes. And God saw to it that forever afterward each tree or bush would bear fruit of its own kind.

By the end of this third day the earth was bursting with color and beauty. Having just created a field of delicate, star-white flowers, God stepped back to watch a tree stretching its branches toward the blue bowl of the sky. His creation pleased Him. "It is good," He said, "very good."

Flamingoes strutted on legs like stilts

On the fourth day, God looked at the vast vault of the empty sky. "That won't do," He thought.

So He spoke the Word, and a great light appeared in the sky to rule the daytime. This dazzling light was the Sun, set close to the earth to warm it.

Opposite the Sun, He set a smaller light, the Moon, with its white and blue shadings, to rule the night.

God spoke again, and the heavenly meadows of blackness sparkled with shining stars, so many that we are still trying to count them. Planets whirled into orbit. God set all the heavenly lights moving in patterns like the works of a great clock. And the sun slid up the sky to begin another day. "That's the way," God decreed, "we shall have day and night, seasons, and years."

On the fifth day the Creator-God looked at the surging seas, the rivers, the brooks, and the sky above, imagining them full of living creatures. Now when He spoke, more marvelous things happened. . . . Feathers fanned . . . beaks squawked . . . fins flapped . . . claws clutched . . . snouts sniffed.

The sea and the sky were astir with new life. Birds, blue as the sky, smoothed their feathers in the maple trees. Tiny humming birds with jeweled colors swooped and darted to suck the sweetness from the hearts of the flowers; canaries and nightingales sang glorious songs. Schools of blue and yellow fish darted through the gently swaying seaweed, and great black whales spouted water high into the air. In the reedy marshes, pink flamingoes strutted about on legs like stilts.

Raising His strong hands over the earth, God blessed all the living creatures in the water and in the sky. "Be fruitful," He said. "Bring forth many little ones just like you."

THE FIRST MAN AND WOMAN

Genesis 1:26–31; 2:7–25

So now the earth was swarming with animals and birds and fish, but the Creator-God was still lonely. For five days He had been building the lovely earth as a home for this new life. Now another kind of creature was needed to enjoy all this beauty and to take care of it.

God wanted this new creature to be greater than the animals and birds and fish, a being who would resemble Him, made in His own image.

Man. . .

The sun shone through the leaves of the fruit trees, filling the Garden of Eden with a cool, green light. The fragrance of many flowers filled the morning air.

God was already at work. Sweeping the dust, God shaped Man. Marvelously, He formed this crown of His creation with a strong body and sturdy arms and legs, giving him a heart to beat, miles of arteries and veins to nourish and cleanse the blood, every tissue and organ needed for a healthful, joyful life.

Not only that, this Man was given a brain better than any animal's so that he would be able to think and plan and choose, to love, and to create beauty. Yes, and to worship. God was making Man so wondrously that he would be able to understand Who had made the animals and the amazing world around him. Understanding that, Man could then know and enjoy his God. The spirit within him, made in the image of God's Spirit, would want to worship so great a Creator. Thus God would never again be lonely.

Birds and beasts watched silently as God knelt over His handiwork, the perfectly formed body of Man, and breathed into it the breath of His own life.

At that moment Man became a living soul whose spirit would live forever.

The new creature yawned, stretched himself, and sat up.

"You will be called 'Adam,'" God told him.

That day God walked all the paths of Eden with Adam. He showed this happy man all the splendors of the garden and where, beside a misty waterfall, the sweetest berries grew.

Adam was full of questions about the earth, the sky, and the waters. Scarcely would God finish answering one question before the man would ask another.

"What is this called?" asked Adam. An enormous, golden-eyed animal with yellow and black stripes had crept from the forest to sniff at him.

God looked at Adam and answered, "Since you are to rule over all these creatures, you must name him. And all the others too."

"Tiger," said Adam. The tiger twitched his tail, pleased with his new name. Each time another animal came to sniff and stare, Adam gave him a name.

"Gorilla." "Duck." "Cat." "Sparrow." "Snake." "Mouse." By the end of the day, Adam had named all the animals.

The evening fireflies were blinking in the grass when Adam sat down to rest. Something was puzzling him. Among all the creatures there was not one that looked like him.

He leaned back in a thick carpet of moss, and was about to ask God about this. But God had already planned one more special gift for Adam.

God caused Adam to fall into a deep, deep sleep.

Once more, God knelt over the Man. Carefully, gently, He took a rib from Adam's side as he slept. The evening breezes rustled in the leaves of the trees, and an owl called out as God worked, fashioning for Adam a beautiful companion.

When God finished, He shook Adam to wake him. Adam saw the new creature at once. She was watching him with tender, dark eyes, and he fell in love with her at first sight.

Standing up, Adam took her hands. "Your name is Eve," he

said. "And I am Adam. You will be called Woman because you were taken from Man. You will be the mother of all mankind."

So Eve became Adam's wife, just as God had planned. God blessed them right there in the garden before all the animals and birds, as the two stood hand in hand in the golden sunlight.

"Be fruitful and multiply," God told them. "Fill all the earth with your little ones. Because you are both made in My image, I now give you authority over the fish of the sea, the birds of the air, the beasts of the field. You may rule the whole earth."

All the animals had crept around the clearing to watch, and they twitched their tails for joy. All except the snake. He did not like the thought of anyone ruling over him.

By the seventh day God had ended His work. The world was warmed by the sun and slept under the moon; the world was alive and Man reigned over it.

God said, "What I did, I did well."

Then He rested.

And God blessed in a special way that day He rested: He sanctified it, calling it "the Sabbath."

"Forever afterward, it will be good for Man to follow My example," God said. "He should work for six days and then set aside one day for rest."

In Eden, the beautiful garden that God had planted for Adam and Eve, there were two types of trees. . .

Those heavy with flowers that they would please the eyes.

Those laden with fruits that they would please the lips.

God told Adam, "You will tend the trees and plants and enjoy them. And Eve will always help you."

Adam and Eve were happy in Eden because God had given them each other and so much to enjoy. Not only that, often they

spoke with God, and He with them. He would even walk and talk with them in the cool of the evening.

The Creator's love was all around Adam and Eve. And their love flowed back to this great-hearted, unselfish God who wanted only good for them.

That's why Adam and Eve knew nothing at all about disobedience or fear or evil or wrongdoing or death. And God did not want them to know, for that would spoil their happiness.

Yet God knew that He must warn Adam and Eve. He told them, "You can eat any fruit of any tree in this garden. But keep away from the tree in the middle of the garden. Do not even touch its fruits. For this is the Tree of the Knowledge of Good and Evil. And I, your God, tell you—you shall die if you taste any fruit from this tree."

Adam and Eve stood before God, arm in arm, and vowed, "We will never eat from the forbidden tree. No, never."

ONE TRICKY SNAKE

Genesis 3

Eden was full of life, color, and happiness. Except for one creature named "Snake."

Snake was displeased because God had said that Adam and Eve could rule over him and all the other living creatures. The evil in Snake did not want anybody ruling over him. So a dark plan began forming in his flat, bald head shaped like a triangle.

Snake was waiting for the right moment.

The snake is not only a cunning animal, but a patient one. Finally, one day under the noon sun, the snake came out from under a flat rock. He had seen Eve picking oranges nearby.

Slithering up to Eve, the snake hissed, "Good day, Eve."

Adam and Eve make new friends

Eve was not afraid of the snake since in Eden she had never felt fear.

"Good day, Snake," she answered cheerily.

The snake came closer. "Does God allow you to eat any fruit from any tree in the garden?"

Eve paused in her work. "We can eat from every tree, yes. Except one." She pointed across the field. "God said we must never eat from that one. If we do, we will surely die."

The snake laughed. "Oh no," he lied, leaning closer to her like a friend telling a secret. "In fact, if you eat that fruit, you will be just like God: you will know all about good and evil."

He sounded so convincing that Eve was confused. The snake saw this, so he rushed her along.

"Come with me," he hissed, hurrying through the grass. "You'll see. You won't die. You'll be just like God. I'll show you."

Eve felt a twisting, worried knot in her stomach. Deep down she realized that the loving God she knew so well would never lie to her; also that it was wrong to disobey Him. Yet suddenly she wanted more than anything else to taste that forbidden fruit.

Eve was just about to run after the snake when Adam walked up the shady garden path.

"Hurry, Adam," she said, grabbing his arm. "The snake has something good for us. We'll be just like God. You'll see. Come."

Through the garden they ran, into the clearing where the forbidden tree stood. God had called it the Tree of the Knowledge of Good and Evil. No birds nested in its branches. Its ripe, round fruit filled the clearing with a sweet smell.

Eve plucked one of the fruits, bit it, but found it horribly sour. At once Eve knew she had made a terrible mistake.

Adam was astonished. "Eve. What have you *done?* This is the forbidden tree!"

The first temptation

Eve had never felt so strange—and guilty. "If only Adam would eat the fruit too," she thought, "then I won't feel so terrible and so—so alone."

"You see," she shrugged, "I didn't die. So you won't die either. God must be wrong. The fruit is sweet," she lied to Adam even as the snake had lied to her.

So Adam disobeyed God and tasted the fruit too. He found it not only sour, but bitter. For the first time, fear entered into both Adam and Eve. They stood there, frightened and shaking. Their hearts and minds felt soiled for thinking evil thoughts about God.

Then, for the first time, they realized that they were naked and were ashamed to look at each other. So they hid in the bushes.

Snake was nowhere to be found.

At dusk, God came into the Garden, searching for Adam and Eve. They were still in the bushes, trembling.

"Adam? Eve?" He called. "Why are you hiding from Me?"

"We're hiding because we're naked," cried Adam.

"Who told you that you were naked?" God asked, His voice sad and stern. "Have you eaten the fruit of the tree which gives the knowledge of good and evil?"

"Yes, my Lord God, I have eaten of the forbidden fruit," Adam replied.

Then Adam and Eve crept from the bushes, both talking at once.

"Lord she made me eat the fruit," Adam said, pointing to Eve.

"It's not my fault," was Eve's retort. "Snake made me eat it."

God made no answer for a moment, just turned away, sad that evil had entered Man's perfect Garden-home.

Later on He summoned the snake. "Because you have lied

to this woman, you have brought a curse on all living things. But you are cursed most of all. From now on, you will forever slither your way across the earth, crawling on your belly with dust in your mouth. You and all your children will be the enemy of Man.''

To Eve, God said, ''From now on, childbirth will cause you great pain. Instead of you telling your husband what to do, he shall be your head and your happiness shall depend on him.''

And to Adam, ''You have obeyed your wife rather than obeying Me. Now you'll have to sweat and battle the thorns and thistles and weeds to raise your food. Because of you, death of the body has come to the earth. You were made of dust, and your body will return to the ground at the end of your days.''

Eden was now a sad place. The animals fought and killed each other. So God took their skins and made clothes for Adam and Eve because they were ashamed of their nakedness.

Finally, God told Adam and Eve that they must leave Eden. He led them to the edge of the Garden and set them walking into the wilderness.

When Adam and Eve had walked a little way, they turned to look back longingly at their Garden-home. But the gate was now shut; an angel with a fiery sword stood barring the path.

Not only that, a thick night had fallen upon Eden. Great was God's wrath that His beautiful creation had been spoiled by evil.

Adam and Eve knew that they could never go back.

What they did not know was that God's power is *always* greater than Snake's. So even as heartbroken Adam and Eve were fleeing, God was at work on a Master Plan: later on, Snake's neck would be crushed. God would then restore to all humans who want it another kind of Eden.

Today the gates of this new Garden are wide open to every child and man and woman who wants God's light and truth and joy instead of Snake's dark ways.

A JEALOUS BROTHER

Genesis 4

Adam and Eve now lived in the wilderness outside Eden.

Here the fruit trees grew tangled and sour. Vegetables and flowers fought to push up through the rocky soil and thorns. Just to raise some food to eat, Adam had to work for long hours each day under the hot sun, plowing and planting.

At night he had to guard his flocks of cattle, sheep, and goats, for the wolves and lions were wild and fierce. They lurked in shadowy forests, waiting to pounce on a stray lamb or calf.

From Adam's and Eve's love for each other was born a first child: a boy they named Cain. Then another son was born—Abel.

When Cain was a boy, Adam took him out to the fields and taught him to plow and plant and tend the fruit trees. He grew up to become a farmer, and was very proud of his fields and orchards.

In the same way, Adam taught Abel to become a good herdsman. He learned to fight the wild beasts that came to steal his young, tender lambs. Abel loved his quiet flocks.

One morning Cain and Abel were walking together through the ripening fields.

"Let's take a gift to the Lord," said Cain. "He'll be pleased to see how hard we've worked."

"Yes," said Abel. "You can give some of your crops, and I'll give Him some animals.

So Cain gathered a few bushels of figs, sweet melons, and vegetables as his gift for the Lord.

Abel however, decided to give the Lord what he loved most of all, three of his fat, woolly lambs.

When the brothers took their gifts to the Lord, He was very pleased. Cain set down bushels of fruits and vegetables and beamed with pride. Then Abel presented his young, snowy-white lambs. But there was sadness in his eyes as he stroked their little heads.

God's heart was touched when He saw how much Abel loved the lambs, but that even so he was offering them as a gift.

"You have given me such a special gift, Abel," He said.

Immediately, Cain was jealous. His face clouded with anger. "My gifts are just as good as Abel's," he complained.

"Why are you angry?" asked God. "Aren't your gifts accepted when you've done well? Be careful though, for I see evil creeping into your heart."

But Cain could not control his anger. Later he strode to the meadow where Abel was tending his flocks and crept up behind his brother. Using a heavy rock, Cain struck Abel with all his strength. Abel fell to the earth—dead.

When Cain tried to slip stealthily away, God met him on the path.

"Where is Abel, your brother?" He asked Cain.

Cain could not face God. "I'm not my brother's keeper," was his answer.

God led Cain to the red earth where Abel had fallen. "Your brother's blood cries out to Me from the ground," He said sternly.

"By killing your own brother, you have brought a fearful curse upon yourself," God went on. "From now on the soil will no longer yield its fruit to you. And you shall wander without end, always running in fear of men."

Cain hung his head in shame, his voice trembling. "Now everyone will try to kill me. I won't have a home," he cried miserably.

God's heart was moved with pity. He reached out His hand and placed a mark on Cain as a sign.

"No one will kill you when they see My mark. If anyone harms you, their punishment will be seven times greater."

So Cain left his home, his fields, and his mother and father. He wandered until he came to the land of Nod, east of Eden.

There Cain found a wife who bore him a son called Enoch.

Adam andd Eve now had lost both of their sons. They were heartbroken. But God blessed them with another child. And they named him Seth.

THE BIGGEST FLOOD
Genesis 6:5–8:22

In time, the whole earth was filled with people. All men and women were of the family of Adam and Eve.

But it was not a happy world. Brothers fought. Men stole from one another, even from poor widows. Children lied and disobeyed their parents. Young men killed to get what they wanted.

God saw all this evil. It grieved His loving heart. The world would have to be punished.

But God always looks for goodness in people. Such goodness He saw in a man named Noah. Noah loved God. Every day he would thank God for his blessings, especially for his wife and family.

This good man also taught his three sons—Shem, Ham, and Japheth—and their wives all about God, and they worshipped Him together at a stone altar Noah had built.

At night, as they ate by a crackling fire, Noah would point to the stars. "See all those stars? God created every one of them." Then Noah would tell his family about Eden and about Adam and Eve. All this wonderful knowledge had been passed down from father to son for many years.

Noah's wicked neighbors scoffed. "There's no God. No one has ever *seen* Him. You're just a fool, Noah."

But Noah and his family were faithful and believed.

One day, while Noah was busy at work in his vineyards, the Lord appeared. "Noah, wickedness flows from men's hearts like

a river. Therefore, I am going to send a great flood on earth to destroy it. All living creatures will die.

"But I will spare you and your family because I have seen the goodness in your heart. It shines like a light in the wicked world.

"For forty days and forty nights it will rain. The heavens will pour like waterfalls. Waves will cover the mountains, even the highest peaks. To escape this punishment, you and your sons must build a huge ark of cypress wood."

Then God told Noah exactly how high and wide and long to build the ark—because no one had ever before built such a boat. It was to have three stories, with a window near the top.

Noah and his sons set to work. They felled huge trees, smoothing them into beams and planks. With thick tar they painted the ark inside and out. Everything was done just as the Lord told them.

As the work was being done, Noah's wicked neighbors would come by, making fun of Noah and his sons. "God talked to you, did He? Our crazy Noah now hears voices. Who ever heard of building a ship on *dry* land?"

But Noah's family kept right on believing God and working.

After many, many weeks of hard work, the ark was ready.

God now spoke to Noah again. "You are to take into the ark with you two of every sort of bird and animal and creeping thing living on earth, one male and one female. This way, all the creatures I have made will continue on the earth.

"Also, take with you enough food for all the people and animals."

Soon the ark was alive with sound. Monkey's chattered. Birds sang. Dogs barked. Cows mooed.

Noah led the last slow, clumsy elephants to their stall just as the sky began to darken.

As the neighbors stood around watching and jeering, black thunderclouds gathered above them. The wind began to whip raindrops in their faces.

Then God Himself closed the door of the ark.

Clouds emptied rain upon the earth. Lightning ripped the sky. Rivers and lakes overflowed their banks, flooding plains and valleys.

Men and women ran for shelter. At first they thought, "Oh, it's just a bad storm. The sun will shine again tomorrow."

But the next day water was still streaming down. And the next . . . and the next. Soon the earth looked like an endless lake.

The storm raged on and on for forty days and forty nights. Inside the ark Noah's family were frightened but safe. They did all they could to keep the animals calm. Outside, the waters rose and rose, covering everything.

All of the wicked people drowned. Every living thing on earth died except those in the ark.

Finally, the storm stopped. Noah and his family looked from the window, but they could see only blue sky and green sea— no earth, no mountains, no trees.

Then God ordered the wind, "Blow on the earth to dry up the waters."

After several months, Noah opened a window and set free a dove to fly over the waters. But the dove found no dry place to land and soon returned to the ark.

In a week, he released another dove. She came back in the evening with an olive sprig in her beak. That meant that somewhere dry ground had appeared.

Another week went by and Noah set free a third dove. She did not return.

"She's found dry land," Noah rejoiced, "and a place to build her nest."

At last the ark came to rest on a mountain peak. Noah opened the great doors. Outside, the golden light was bright with hope, and around the big ark the earth was dry.

A rainbow to remember

Noah called his family together and said, "We can now leave the ark and take the animals with us. Outside, we will rejoice, giving thanks to God, our Lord."

Men, women, and animals crowded out of the ark, the animals sniffing at the newly washed earth.

Before he did anything else, Noah built an altar of stones and offered a sacrifice to God to thank Him for saving his family and the animals from the flood.

As Noah and his family knelt in worship, God spoke to them, "Noah, I will make a Covenant with you and with all men and women who live on the earth from now on: never again will I destroy the earth with a flood. I'm giving you and all men always a sign that I *will* keep My promise."

Looking up, they saw a beautiful bow being drawn across the sky. Blue, green, yellow, orange, red it glowed—a gorgeous rainbow.

"Whenever you see this sign after a rain, you will take this as the sign of My promise," God said.

And today when you too see a rainbow after a rain, you will remember that God always keeps His promises.

God blessed Noah, and he lived to be nine hundred and fifty years old. He saw his sons grow, and his grandsons, and his great-grandsons. He told them all about the flood, and God's promise, and the rainbow.

And in time the earth was filled with people once again.

A TOWER THAT TOUCHED THE CLOUDS

Genesis 11:1–9

At one time, all of Noah's descendants spoke one language. Almost too many to be counted, they spread across the earth and built splendid cities.

The tower was too tall

Some of the people wandered to the country of Shinar. They settled in tents on a wide plain covered with cypress and palm trees where there were many bubbling springs.

"Let's build a city of our own called 'Babel,'" they said. "It will be the greatest of all cities under heaven."

They were full of pride. At night you could hear them whispering, "Our beautiful city will be so huge that it will be seen from all over the universe. And at its center we will build a tower so high that it will reach the sky."

They felt they could do this because they had discovered how to make bricks: by mixing clay and water and laying them under the sun until baked dry. These bricks enabled them to make buildings higher than anyone had seen before.

So workmen gathered clay from the riverbanks and began pressing it into bricks. Woodcarvers worked on wooden ornaments to decorate the buildings.

The people were excited. "Yes! We can reach heaven itself with our tower," they shouted.

All day the workers molded bricks, bricks, and more bricks for the tower. Others hauled buckets of slime to use as mortar between the bricks. Still others assembled the bricks and laid them, one upon the other.

Row by row, brick by brick, the Tower of Babel grew upwards.

It grew above the rooftops of the city.

Soon the tower was taller than the cypress and palm trees, then higher than the birds could fly, until, at last, the top was lost in the clouds.

As the tower grew, the people of Babel grew more and more proud and haughty. They boasted to everyone who came into the city, "We can reach heaven itself merely by climbing our tower."

All this time God had been watching the tower grow. He also was seeing the terrible pride growing in the hearts of the people.

And God thought, "If they raise this tower too high, they will begin to think that they are gods. And how could men filled with so much pride have love for Me and for other people? Instead, they will destroy each other."

Of course, God could have reached out one finger and toppled the Tower of Babel. But solving the problem that way would not have ended the pride and conceit and greed in the peoples' hearts.

Therefore, God chose another way . . . and His ways are not our human ways; God's ways are always so much better than ours.

So what did God do? He reached out His finger and touched the tongues of everyone in the city of Babel.

Then suddenly each person was speaking a different language. People could no longer understand each other.

In the streets, children stopped their play. Now no one could understand the games. At the market, no one could buy or sell because nobody could agree on the price.

At the tower, one man would give an order; another would shake his head.

Very soon, since they could no longer talk to each other, work on the tower stopped altogether.

Because they could no longer talk to their neighbors, most of the citizens of Babel decided to move away. Soon they scattered over the face of the earth.

Day after day the Tower of Babel stood empty of people, drying up under the sun. Night after night, sand storms swept the bricks crumbling them. No men came near it. Snakes and birds took over the tower as a refuge.

What had been dust was fast becoming dust again. When Man works only to please himself and not to glorify God, what he builds does not last.

THE FATHER WHO OBEYED

Genesis 12:1–8; 13:5–18; 21:1–7; 22:1–18

Abraham and his wife, Sarah, lived alone in their tent of goatskins in the land of Haran. The fact that they had no children made them sad.

Yet Abraham's faith in God was very strong. Though many others in the land worshipped false gods—images made of stone or wood or metal—to Abraham this seemed foolish. For Abraham knew the real God, the God who had made the world and who could perform miracles.

But faith is like an anchor holding a boat. You never know how strong faith really is until a storm comes along and tests its strength.

One hot afternoon the Lord appeared to Abraham and spoke. . . "Abraham, I want you to leave the land of your fathers. I will lead you to a new land which I will give you. And though you have no children now, I will make you the father of a mighty nation."

"Me? You mean *me,* Lord? How can I be the father of many when I'm not even the father of one child? Sarah and I are much too old to have children now."

God did not answer. He had given Abraham His Word. Now it was up to Abraham to believe God and obey—or not. As Abraham pondered what God had said, he decided to trust Him. He went immediately to tell Sarah.

"The Lord is going to give us a new land," he announced happily. "Pack up the tents and all our belongings. Harness the camels and donkeys. Prepare the servants. We are leaving tomorrow for our new home."

It was a long caravan. Abraham took the lead of it, draped in his long coat, listening for the Lord's directions. Camels laden with yellow and red bundles plodded over the hot, sandy hills.

They went through kingdoms and kingdoms, some rich and fertile, ruled by kings who wore golden rings on each finger.

Camels plodded over sandy hills

Sometimes Abraham felt so tired he wanted to give up, but God continued to speak softly in Abraham's ear. "No stopping yet. I will show you the place."

One evening just before sunset, the caravan climbed to the crest of a steep hill. A beautiful land, with winding streams running through it, stretched out before them, fading into a distant blue. There was something special about this place! Abraham's heart leapt within him for joy.

Then God spoke to Abraham through the clear evening sky. "As far as you can see to the north, south, east, and west, I give this land to you."

As night came on, the Lord directed, "Look up at all the stars, Abraham. There are more than you could ever count. I promise that you will have as many descendants as the stars that burn in the sky."

Early the next day, Abraham drove his caravan down into the new land. The herds stopped to graze in deep, sweet grass. They would go no further; this would be home.

Abraham and Sarah pitched their goatskin tent in the shade of tall trees near a flowing spring. They lived there for many years. Still they had no child. The Lord was testing Abraham's faith.

The Lord visited Abraham again one day. As they sat on a rock talking, Abraham asked, "Lord, how am I to become the father of a great nation? I am old now and still have no son. Are my servants going to inherit all this land?"

Again the Lord gave His promise. "Sarah *will* have a son."

Sarah was hiding at the door of the tent, listening. She laughed to herself. "I did not have children when I was a young wife. How can I have a son now that I am old and withered?"

But when Sarah was ninety years old, she did have a son. He was one of God's miracle-children. The Lord told Abraham to name the boy Isaac, which means "laughter."

"The Lord has turned my childless sorrow into joy," said Sarah. Abraham had never been so happy.

Isaac was a strong, healthy boy. He tended the flocks with Abraham, and they would spend day after day together in the hills.

Now God knew that Abraham could not become the head of a great nation unless Abraham trusted God's love completely: he would have to be willing to obey God even if God asked him to do something that seemed foolish or wrong. For had not sin and sorrow and death first entered the world in the Garden of Eden because the Snake had persuaded Eve and Adam *not* to trust and believe God?

So now God knew that Abraham's faith was ready for the hardest test of all.

One morning God called Abraham. "You are to go on a journey with your son Isaac, your only son whom you love more than yourself."

Abraham bowed.

"And where shall I take the child, my Lord?"

God said, "Up to the top of Mount Moriah. There, when I tell you that the moment has come, you shall make a sacrifice of Isaac."

Icy fear fell on Abraham's heart. Kill his own son? How could he ever do that, even if it was a sacrifice to God?

Of course, Abraham knew that some in his land who worshiped statues *did* sometimes sacrifice babies and little children. But would a God of love ask *that?*

Yet Abraham's desire for obedience was greater than his suffering.

So he was up before sunrise the following day with his walking stick in hand. "Come, Isaac," was all he said. He led Isaac across the plains and up the twisting, rocky path of Mount Moriah. His heart was set on obeying the Lord.

What Abraham did not know was that the minute we decide

to obey God, His loving answer is already on the way. So even as father and son had begun climbing up one side of Mount Moriah, God has started a ram up the other side to meet Abraham at exactly the right moment.

At the top Abraham stopped to build an altar while Isaac helped gather stones and firewood. Isaac was full of questions. "Father, where is the ram for our sacrifice?"

Abraham did not know how to answer. With deep anguish he bound Isaac hand and foot and laid him across the altar. From his leather pack he drew a sharp knife, holding it behind his back for a moment as tears clouded his old eyes. He prayed silently, "Lord, I don't understand why my son must die. I love him more than my own life. Still, I will do what You ask."

Now God knew for certain that Abraham would obey everything He asked. Abraham's faith had proven true. God already had one of His heavenly angels there. "Stop Abraham's hand before he lifts the knife," He ordered.

The angel split the air like a fiery bolt of lightning and stopped Abraham's hand.

"You have obeyed the Lord's command," declared the angel. "Unbind Isaac. Now you, Abraham, will be honored through all time for your trust in God."

Father and son hugged each other and danced for joy.

"Look, Father!" Isaac was pointing to a bush. There was the ram, the one God had sent up the other side of the mountain, struggling, its horns tangled in a young thorn tree.

After sacrificing the ram to the Lord, father and son climbed down the mountain, laughing together and singing all the way. Abraham walked like a young man again, with a spring in his step.

Abraham and Sarah lived to be very old. Isaac was a mature man when his father died.

He married a beautiful young girl, Rebekah, from the city of Nahor.

Isaac trusted God all his life, just as his father had taught him. He could never forget what had happened on Mount Moriah to show him how much God blesses us when we obey Him.

TWIN BROTHERS WHO HATED EACH OTHER

Genesis 25:19–34; 27; 28; 32; 33

Jacob and Esau were the twin sons of Isaac. It was strange the way they were born. Esau came first, then Jacob followed, holding on to Esau's heel.

But the brothers were not close as they grew up. Esau was easygoing with red hair even on his arms and body, and loved to spend his days hunting. Though he cared little about family customs and religious life, and even took two pagan Hittite women as his wives, Esau was still his father's favorite son.

Jacob was the favorite of his mother, Rebekah. He was a peace-loving, thoughtful, and clever son who enjoyed the simple life of his home and tending to the herds.

It was the custom in those days that upon the death of the father, the oldest son would inherit twice as many family possessions as the other sons. This was called the oldest son's "birthright." Though Esau expected to receive that and also his father's blessing as head of the family when old Isaac died, it did not seem important to him.

One day Esau returned from hunting, exhausted and very hungry. Jacob was cooking a pot of lentils on an open fire. The good smell of it made Esau demand, "Give me some of that food. I'm starving."

Jacob studied his brother. "Would you trade your birthright for a good meal?"

Angels climbed up and down the ladder

"You can have it," the hungry hunter agreed. "All you'll get for it is a wilderness full of snakes and scorpions. Even the hunting is terrible."

Jacob was astonished that Esau would give up his birthright for so little. Later on he told his mother what had happened.

"My son, now is the time to get your father's blessing," Rebekah said. "Your father is old, blind, and dying. I have a plan."

Rebekah fetched a goatskin from her tent. With the coarse, hairy skin covering his arms and chest, Jacob went into the tent where his blind father lay resting.

Jacob knelt beside Isaac. "Father, would you bless me before you die?" he asked, trying to sound like Esau.

Isaac reached out weakly and set his trembling hand on Jacob's arm. Feeling the hairy goatskin, he thought it was Esau.

"Yes, my son, it is time for me to give you my blessing," the old man said. "May God give you the richness of the earth. You are to be lord over your brothers!"

When Esau learned how he had been tricked, he was very angry. He also realized what a fool he had been to sell his birthright to his brother. "When my father dies," he vowed, "I'll kill my brother Jacob."

Isaac was distressed too with Jacob for deceiving him, but there was no way he could withdraw his blessing once he had given it.

When she heard of Esau's threat to kill Jacob, Rebekah was terrified for her favorite son. So she persuaded Jacob to flee to her brother's home far away in Haran.

It was a sad, penitent Jacob who left his home for a long journey by foot through the wilderness. He was sorry now that he had tricked his old father and Esau, and he felt like a coward to be running away from his brother's fury. God saw the sorrow in Jacob's heart for his wrongdoing.

One night, using a large, flat stone as a pillow, Jacob had a dream. He saw a ladder of gold, so tall that it reached heaven. Angels, glowing like the sun, climbed up and down the ladder all night long. But the most extraordinary thing was that God Himself stood at the top of the ladder.

God was looking kindly upon Jacob and saying, ''You *are* the heir to the promises made to Abraham: this land on which you are lying I give to you and to your descendants. They shall be as countless as the dust upon the earth. I am with you and will keep you wherever you go.''

When Jacob awoke he felt comforted and awed. ''The Lord is in this place,'' he said. ''It is the gate of heaven.''

Then he took the stone that he had used to rest his head, poured oil on it to bless the spot, and called it ''Bethel.''

''But Lord,'' he prayed, ''I need something more—peace between me and my brother Esau.''

Jacob settled in Haran. For twenty years he worked for Laban, his uncle. There he married a beautiful girl named Rachel and became a wealthy man with a large family and many herds of his own.

Then it was time to go back to his home and face his brother. Because he was still afraid of Esau's anger, he took with him a peace offering of five hundred animals from his flock.

During the journey Jacob lay down to rest one night beside a brook. Then in the darkness a strange man surrounded by light came across the brook toward Jacob. Jacob was frightened and began to fight the stranger.

All through the night the two men wrestled. It was more than a physical battle. Jacob was also wrestling with himself, his conscience, and the guilt he still felt for deceiving his father and his brother.

The fight went on all night. Toward morning the stranger struck Jacob in his thigh, wounding him.

Still Jacob would not let him go. He was determined to overcome his cowardice and his fearfulness represented by this stranger.

As the sun rose over the eastern hills, the stranger said, "It is daybreak. Let me go."

"Not until you bless me," said Jacob, tightening his grip.

"What is your name?"

"Jacob."

"Well," came the answer, "your new name is 'Israel.' Israel means 'you strove with God.' "

Jacob was amazed. Now he understood: he had been wrestling with one of God's angels. Though wounded, his spirit was strengthened. God was still with him. Did this not mean that things would go well when he met Esau?

That day Jacob hurried on with his long procession of camels and flocks. Then a servant reported that someone was coming toward them with about four hundred men. It was Esau.

Suddenly the old fears returned. Why would Esau have so many with him? Jacob wondered. "Are they going to kill me, my companions, and my children?"

He was tempted to flee. But the struggle with the angel had given Jacob a new courage. He stood his ground and awaited his brother.

Then, to Jacob's astonishment, as soon as Esau saw him, he ran toward him and hugged his brother. Together they wept for joy. God had touched Esau's heart too and taken away his hatred so that the two brothers could now love each other.

THE DREAMER WHO SAVED HIS PEOPLE

Genesis 37:3–36; 39–46:1–6

Jacob (now called Israel) eventually would have a big family—twelve sons in all. The one named Joseph was Israel's favorite. He loved Joseph so much that he gave him a very beautiful coat

Joseph with his sheep

of many colors. This made the ten older brothers very jealous.

Joseph had another special gift, this one given him by God: he was able to tell the meaning of important dreams. This also made his brothers angry because they envied him so much.

One morning Joseph awoke his older brothers very early while there were still a few stars in the sky. "My brothers, I've just got to tell you about a strange dream I had. We were harvesting wheat in a field. As we bound our wheat into sheaves, my sheaf stood right up on end. Your sheaves gathered around and bowed down to my sheaf."

Now this was too much. "Dreamer!" they ranted. "You are only seventeen, and now you think you are going to rule over us. We'll teach you a lesson." So they began to scheme against their brother.

Not many days later Israel called Joseph into his tent. "Your brothers are working far out in the fields. How about taking them some refreshment?"

Joseph left, carrying a skin of cool water for his brothers. While he was still in the distance, they spotted his many-colored coat bobbing through the wheat fields.

"Here comes that 'dreamer.' Now we can get rid of him," they plotted.

When Joseph reached them, the ten brothers circled him and tore off his coat. They hit him with their fists and with sticks and threw him into a pit. Breathless and bruised, Joseph lay in the bottom of the dark hole.

Just then a caravan drew near. Some traders were on their way to Egypt to buy and sell exotic spices, perfumes, and jewels.

"Let's sell Joseph to these traders," said one brother. "We'll be rid of him forever."

So Joseph was hoisted from the pit, bound, and laid across a camel. "He'll bring a handsome price in Egypt," laughed the cruel traders.

The brothers killed a wild beast, dipped Joseph's coat in the blood, and took it home. When they told their father that Joseph

Joseph's dream of the sheaves

had been killed by the wild beast, Israel mourned his son for many, many days.

Down in Egypt, Joseph was sold as a slave in the marketplace. Potiphar, the captain of the guard for King Pharaoh, bought Joseph and led him home in chains.

But God had given Joseph many skills and he gained favor in Potiphar's eyes. When other slaves fought, Joseph made peace among them. When Joseph was sent to market, he spent his master's money wisely. Soon Potiphar gave Joseph charge over all the household duties and the other slaves.

But Joseph's heart still ached with loneliness for his mother and father and brothers.

Once when Potiphar was away at Pharaoh's palace, his wife called Joseph to her bedroom. Joseph was very handsome, and Potiphar's wife thought that she was in love with him. She threw her arms around his neck.

Joseph tried to push away from her. "I cannot sin against God and my master Potiphar," he told her.

It made Potiphar's wife angry to be refused. So she grabbed at Joseph's robe as he twisted away, tearing it off him. Embarrassed, Joseph ran from the room.

Soon afterward, Potiphar returned. His wife, being a very wicked woman, decided to get revenge on Joseph for not doing what she asked. So she showed Joseph's robe to her husband and said, "Look what your favorite slave has done. He came into my room and insulted me, but I silenced him and tore off his robe."

Potiphar, believing that Joseph had tried to steal his wife away from him, had Joseph thrown into Pharaoh's prison. In the cold, damp darkness, Joseph lay on the stinking straw and wept at the unfairness of it all. But even there God was with him and gave him strength.

Two of Pharaoh's own servants, the baker and the butler, were cast into the same prison. Both had strange dreams one night, and in the morning they wondered aloud what the dreams meant.

Joseph said to the butler, "God has shown me the meaning of your dream. In three days you will be proven innocent. Once more you will be head of Pharaoh's household."

It was harder for Joseph to tell the baker what his dream meant because it was bad news. . . "God has also shown me what your dream means. In three days you will be found guilty of your crime. You will be put to death."

And everything came to pass exactly as God had shown Joseph. The baker was executed, but the butler went free. As the guards unlocked his chains, the butler promised Joseph, "I'm going to tell Pharaoh that God is with you and has given you the gift of knowing what dreams mean. Then, surely, Pharaoh will set you free."

But the butler forgot all about his promise. Joseph remained in his cold, wet prison cell for two more years.

One night, God troubled Pharaoh's sleep with a frightening dream. The next day, the King summoned all the magicians and wise men in Egypt to his council room. Then he reported his dream:

"Seven fat cows were eaten by seven thin, sickly cows. I also saw seven ears of corn, full and golden. Seven shriveled ears of corn swallowed them up too."

But not one of the magicians could tell Pharaoh what the dream meant. Then suddenly, the butler remembered Joseph in prison and said to Pharaoh, "In the cell with me in prison there was a young Hebrew named Joseph who would interpret dreams. Why not let him come to you?"

So Joseph was brought before Pharaoh, who told him his dream about the cows and the one about the ears of corn.

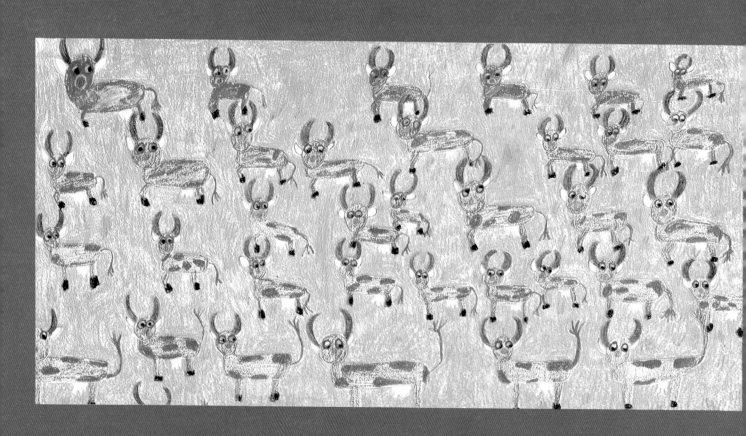

Joseph answered, "The God of heaven and earth has shown me, oh Pharaoh, what your dream means: for seven years Egypt will enjoy bountiful harvests. But after that, this land will be stricken with famine for seven years. You should find a wise man to store up food in the bountiful years of good harvests, or all Egypt will suffer in the famine."

Pharaoh ordered that Joseph's chains be removed at once. "It is clear," he told Joseph, "that your God inspires you, and that your wisdom comes from Him. Would you agree to be the man in charge to prepare for the famine?"

Joseph could scarcely believe his good fortune. Though wrongly held in prison for many months, he had never stopped trusting God. Now, in one day, God had rescued him from prison and made it possible for him to be in charge over all the land of Egypt.

Just as the dream had predicted, for seven years the fields were golden with wheat and corn. Then the famine struck from Egypt all the way to the land of Canaan where Joseph's family lived.

Israel, who was now very old, called his sons together. By now his last son, Benjamin, had been born while Joseph was in Egypt.

"Go down into Egypt and buy some grain," Israel told his sons. "We have none here, and we will soon starve. But Benjamin must stay with me. I would die of sorrow if I lost him as I lost Joseph."

The ten older brothers crossed the burning desert into Egypt. Guards met them at the border and took them straight to Pharaoh's palace where Joseph was in charge of selling grain.

Joseph knew his brothers at once. But they did not recognize Joseph since they thought him long dead. Besides, this grown man robed in royal splendor, did not look at all like the slim young boy they had sold into slavery years before.

"We are starving in Canaan," said the brothers. "Please sell us grain so our poor father and our youngest brother won't die of hunger."

Joseph decided to test his brothers. "Bring your youngest brother here to me. Then I'll sell you grain."

So the brothers travelled back across the desert. After much pleading, they convinced their father to let Benjamin come with them.

At last, all his brothers stood before Joseph again in Pharaoh's palace.

"Fine. Now you may have all the grain you need," agreed Joseph. But as they packed the grain on their camels, Joseph hid a silver cup in Benjamin's bag. Then he summoned the palace guards.

"Look, this boy is stealing from me," he shouted. "Bind him. He will remain in Egypt as my slave. The rest of you may go home."

The ten older brothers fell on their knees before Joseph, pleading. "Our father is old, and will die of grief if we go home without Benjamin. This is our fault. Evil has come upon us for what we did to our brother Joseph long ago."

Joseph loved his father so much he could no longer pretend with his brothers. He wept as he spoke. . .

"I am Joseph, your brother. You meant to harm me, but see how God turned your evil plan into good. I was able to save Egypt from the famine, and now I can save our family too. Go home and bring our father here to Egypt. I shall see to it that all of us will be safe here and well fed."

So Israel travelled to Egypt. "My son is alive!" he exclaimed, hugging Joseph, overcome with joy.

That was the way Israel and all his sons and his entire household escaped the terrible famine. And they lived there in Egypt as special guests of the great Pharaoh.

A BABY IS RESCUED

Exodus 1:1–7:6

The twelve sons of Israel lived in Egypt for many years. Each son's family grew into a large tribe. Together, they worshipped the God of heaven and earth.

Soon after Joseph and his brothers had all died, a new Pharaoh who had not known Joseph, mounted the throne. He called counselors to his throne room and said to them, ''The Hebrews are a threat to us. Soon there are going to be more of them than of us. Then the Hebrews will try to rule us Egyptians. So this is my order: make life very hard for them. Set them to building temples and cities and put cruel taskmasters over them.''

But despite all this harsh treatment, the Hebrews remained strong and had many children.

Finally, the new Pharaoh gave a second edict. . . ''Each time a Hebrew shall have a male child, you shall seize the child and throw him into the Nile to drown or to be eaten by the crocodiles.''

So the soldiers went out to snatch Hebrew baby boys right out of the arms of their weeping mothers.

But one young mother escaped the soldiers. Down a path she ran, straight to the river Nile. She brought with her a waterproof basket made of reeds, and laid her sleeping child in it. The basket rocked gently on the water. Then the girl slipped away, putting her trust in God to save her baby.

Later on that morning, Pharaoh's daughter was bathing in the Nile. On the banks stood her many handmaidens, bearing scented oils for her skin and robes of shining silk. The princess of Egypt spied the floating basket.

''Oh, look! A baby!'' she cried, lifting the child from the basket. ''How beautiful is this Hebrew child. I cannot obey my father's orders and drown such a fine boy. Go," she said to her servant, "find a wet nurse to suckle him, and do not tell anyone about this." For a moment she looked at the baby boy. "I will call him 'Moses,' which means 'drawn from the waters.'"

So that is how Moses was reared in Egypt as the princess' own son. Yet Moses did not grow up to be like the Egyptian boys around him. Always he knew that he was a Hebrew. As he grew older he became very upset because his people suffered so much.

One day, when Moses was a young man, he passed by a quarry where Hebrew slaves were cutting stones. An Egyptian was cruelly lashing a Hebrew on his bare back with leather thongs. In anger, Moses struck the Egyptian hard, killing him.

When Pharaoh heard the news, he declared, "Moses must die."

But Moses escaped. He fled into the wilderness of Midian and hid in the mountains.

For many years Moses lived as a shepherd. He married one of the daughters of the priest of Midian, and expected to spend the rest of his life there.

The Pharaoh who had ordered Moses killed, then died himself.

This Pharaoh's death awakened the people of Israel. They gathered together to pray to the Lord God. . . "Lord, we are slaves who have suffered harsh punishment. Have You forgotten that You made a covenant with our fathers, Abraham, Isaac, and Jacob?"

God heard the prayer of Israel. "It is true," He answered, "that I made a covenant with Abraham, Isaac, and Jacob. Always I keep My covenant-promises. You *will* be delivered."

And Moses was the man God chose to deliver Israel from Egypt and from the new and even harsher Pharaoh.

This is how it happened. . .

One evening, as Moses was driving his flocks home, he heard God calling to him. He looked around and saw a strange sight.

Nearby, a bush was burning with a bright red fire. But when he looked closer, the leaves and branches were not even scorched.

"Moses," God's voice spoke from the burning bush, "I have heard my children crying in Egypt. Go down to that land and tell Pharaoh to let My people go free."

"But I have no power with Pharaoh," Moses objected.

"Have no fear," the Lord replied. "You will stretch out your shepherd's staff, and My own power will cause mighty miracles to happen."

So Moses took with him Aaron, his brother, and they travelled across the windy deserts to Egypt. In Moses' hand was nothing but that shepherd's staff to defend him from all the armies and powers of Egypt.

LET MY PEOPLE GO

Exodus 7:7–12

The mighty Pharaoh sat in his pillared temple. Hundreds of servants stood by, waiting to carry out his slightest wish.

Moses and Aaron squeezed through the crowded courtroom.

Moses knew how to act before Pharaoh since he had been reared by a princess. Yet he and Aaron would not bow down and worship Pharaoh as a god as the Egyptians did.

Instead, with a voice of authority, Moses spoke, "Oh, great Pharaoh, the true God of heaven and of earth says, 'Let My people go.' "

The man on the throne only laughed. "Certainly not. I don't know your God, and I do not believe in Him. All I see is that the people of Israel are trying to escape their work. Therefore they shall be punished more severely than ever."

At that moment, God told Aaron to throw his shepherd's staff down at Pharaoh's feet. Instantly, it turned into a venomous snake.

Pharaoh's court magicians crowded around. "That's nothing. We can do tricks like that."

So using their black arts, they called forth many snakes. But Aaron's snake swallowed up all the others.

Pharaoh was not impressed. "Is that all your God can do?"

One morning Moses went to Pharaoh as he was strolling along the banks of the Nile. The waters were, on that particular morning, a most beautiful shade of blue.

Moses pleaded with Pharaoh. "Why are you deaf? It is God who orders you through my voice to let His people go. And here is the proof!"

He struck the waters with his staff, and instantly, the water was turned into blood. All the fish died, and soon, a dreadful stench spread over the land of Egypt.

Pharaoh summoned the magicians of his kingdom and bid them accomplish the same wonder; so they too turned the pure water into ill-smelling blood.

Triumphantly, Pharaoh ordered Moses out of his sight.

One week later Moses and Aaron stood before Pharaoh again. "Our God is giving you another chance, O Pharaoh. He says, 'Let My people go! If not, I will strike Egypt with plagues.'"

Pharaoh only laughed. "*Never* will I let your people go."

So God sent a plague of frogs upon Egypt. Frogs were everywhere, climbing, hopping, croaking. They hid in pots and baskets. They died in the hot sun and made a sickening smell. Frogs crawled into Pharaoh's bed of carved ivory and even into his shirt.

"Ask your God to take away the frogs," Pharaoh begged. "Then I'll let the Hebrews go free."

So Moses prayed to God, and the frogs disappeared. "*Now* do you believe?" he asked.

But Pharaoh had been lying. "No, I don't believe, and I will not let the Hebrews go," came the cold-hearted answer.

God sent six more plagues upon Egypt. Swarms of buzzing gnats flew in the eyes and noses of the Egyptians. Cattle died in the fields. Festering boils broke out on the people. Hail fell and destroyed the crops, and locusts came soon afterwards to devour what little was left in the fields. Thick darkness covered the entire land, so that everyone stumbled about in confusion.

Yet not one of these terrible plagues came upon the Hebrews because God's hand protected them, their children, and their tents.

After each plague, Pharaoh pretended that he would let the Hebrews go free. But he never meant to keep his promise. Each time God stopped the plague, Pharaoh would again declare, "I will never let the Hebrews go."

Pharaoh's magicians call forth their snakes

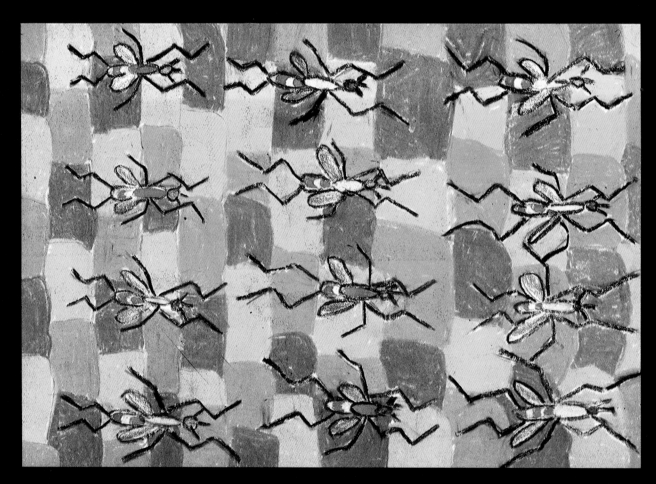

At last God said to Moses, "I must deal very harshly with the Egyptians. Tonight the oldest child of every Egyptian family will die. But My people must sprinkle the blood of a lamb on the doorpost of their home, and their little ones will live."

So during that dark night, the oldest child of every Egyptian family did die. By the time a gray dawn streaked the sky, a mournful wail was heard from nearly every Egyptian home in the land.

But the Hebrews awoke to a joyful day. They stood in the streets with their belongings packed on carts and camels, for they knew freedom was at hand.

Pharaoh summoned Moses. His eyes were red from weeping, for his oldest son too had died during the night.

"Leave, Moses, and take with you all the people of Israel. And pray to your God, Moses, that He will withhold His vengeance," he added bitterly.

The Hebrews cheered and played their tambourines as Moses led them away from the Egyptian cities to the land of Canaan, which the Lord promised to give them. Their singing echoed in the hills as they danced into the wilderness.

But when the Hebrews were out of the city, Pharaoh began to feel that he had been fooled. "We acted in fear without thinking. Who will build my glorious cities now? Who will draw our water, farm our fields, and wait on us? Gather immediately all our war chariots and our best charioteers," the king told his counselors. "I, Pharaoh, will ride at their head. And we'll bring back the slave people before they get away."

The bugs and frogs even crawled into Pharaoh's bed   *The chase begins*

WALK THROUGH THE SEA

Exodus 13:17–22; 14

But Moses and his people had a good start. At the end of the first day they reached the Red Sea as the evening shadows purpled the western hills. There the Hebrews were about to pitch their tents for the night.

Then someone shouted, "Look behind us. That cloud of dust! The Egyptians are chasing us with chariots and horses. We're trapped here by the sea."

At that instant, God spoke to Moses. "Lift up your shepherd's staff and stretch it over the sea."

As Moses did so, the waters flowed back and separated. There, between the foaming waves, was a narrow canyon, leaving a dry path across the sea to the other shore.

"Hurry!" called Moses. The Hebrews, with their children and carts, fled along the dry sea bottom, walls of water glistening and splashing far above their heads. All reached the other side safely.

By now the Egyptian horses and chariots had caught up and were chasing after them on the same dry path through the Red Sea.

Once again God called Moses. "Stretch out your hand over the sea. Let the waters flow back over the sea. Let the waters flow back over Pharaoh."

So Moses stretched out his hand, and the walls of water crashed back into the seabed, swallowing the entire Egyptian army. There was a dreadful tangle of chariots and men and horses. Not one man or animal was left alive.

Yet all the children of Israel had been saved. Then the descendants of Abraham, Isaac, and Jacob knew that their God keeps His promises. They fell to their knees on the sand of the seashore and sang a hymn of praise to their Lord.

"After them!" shout Pharaoh's generals

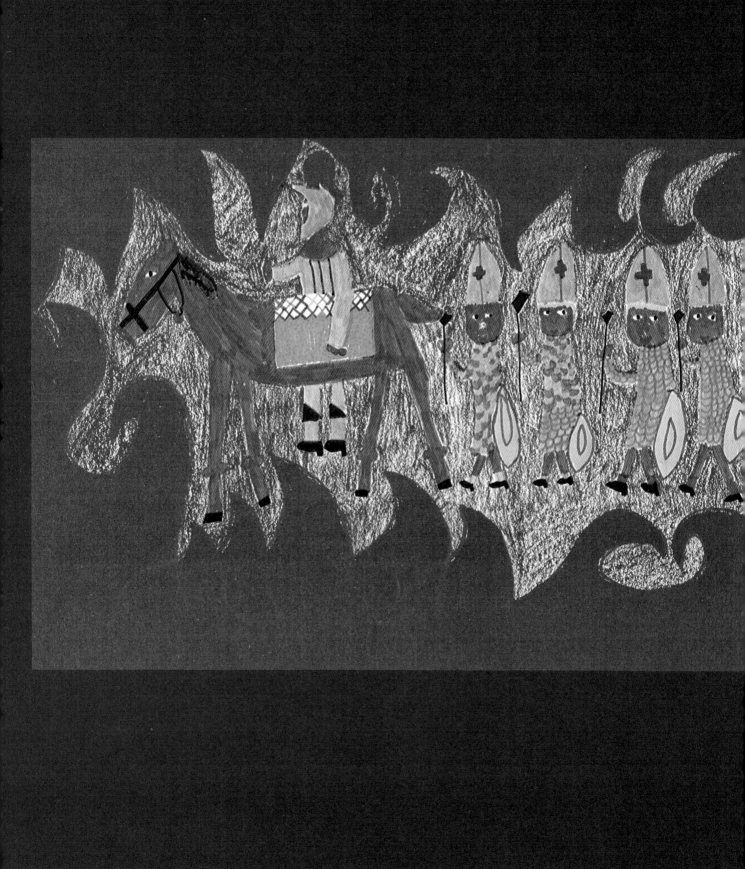

The next day, as the Hebrews began their long journey, they found that the Lord Himself was showing them the way to travel through the wilderness. A pillar of smoke moved ahead of them by day, and a pillar of fire led them by night.

"I am leading you to the Promised Land," God told them.

GOD'S THUNDERCLAP

Exodus 15:22–27; 16; 19; 20; 32; Numbers 13; 14; Deuteronomy 34

Many days after leaving Egypt on their way to the Promised Land, the people of Israel reached the vast desert of Shur. The days were sizzling-hot while the nights were icy-cold.

The food brought from Egypt was now gone, and the people were very hungry.

Children cried, women grumbled, men were angry at Moses. They said, "It is true, in Egypt we were slaves. But at least we had enough to eat. In this desert we are free, but we are going to die of starvation."

Moses went off alone to pray. "Lord, these people need food."

The Lord replied, "I will feed them with My own hand."

So God sent down upon the desert a miraculous dew. It tasted like a wafer made with honey, and the people named it "manna." Each night the manna would rain from heaven and every morning the people would gather it.

But soon the Hebrews grew tired of the manna. Some began whispering among themselves. Then others would pick up the complaint. . . "We should have stayed in Egypt where we had meat to eat. God is going to starve us to death with this stuff."

God heard their grumbling, and sent a flock of quail into the camp. The people caught them in nets. In a short time, the aroma of roasting quail filled the air.

Again, the Hebrews were contented for a few days. But even the quail and the manna were not enough for them. "Let's go back to Egypt," they fussed. "It's better to have plenty to eat than our freedom, even the freedom to worship God."

By now it was the third month since the Hebrews had left Egypt.

They were camping near a fast-flowing stream beside a high, rocky mountain named "Sinai."

One morning God said to Moses, "Moses, you saw how I have protected My people. If you follow My laws, you shall be My people among all the peoples on earth. On the day after tomorrow you shall climb alone to the top of this mountain, and I shall speak to you in a special way."

Two mornings later a thick cloud hid the top of Mount Sinai. The people trembled as peal after peal of thunder shook the mountain. Zigzag lightning streaked the sky. The mountain seemed to be smoking.

But Moses was not afraid. "What the Lord God tells us is always for *our* good, to help *us*," he told the people. "I go now to get His special message."

Far up the towering mountainside, the Lord appeared to Moses. His glory shone as such a piercing white light that Moses had

For forty years the Hebrews wandered through the desert

to shield his eyes from the brightness. There, God told Moses, "My people need laws to govern them. I am giving them My commandments, and these will be not just for the Hebrews, but for all people for all time."

Moses watched as the Lord carved ten commandments in tablets of stone:

1. "I am the Lord your God. You shall have no other gods before Me.

2. "You shall not bow down and worship any image made by your own hands.

3. "You shall not use the name of your God disrespectfully.

4. "Remember that the Sabbath day is to be kept. You are to do your work in six days and rest on the Sabbath.

5. "Honor your father and mother that you may live a long and good life.

6. "You shall not murder.

7. "You shall not commit adultery.

8. "You shall not steal.

9. "You shall not lie or ever spread wrong tales about others.

10. "You shall not envy your neighbor, and want to take his home or his wife or anything that belongs to your neighbor."*

* This is a paraphrase for children of the Ten Commandments in the King James Version.

God's glory

Moses remained on the mountain such a long time listening to God that the waiting people grew impatient.

"Moses must be lost or dead," they thought, "and perhaps God is angry with us and has deserted us. Let's make an idol—a calf of gold—and that will be our god."

So they took off their golden earrings, bracelets, necklaces, brooches and rings. They built a furnace and heated it white hot. In it they melted their gold, and formed it into the image of a calf. Aaron, Moses' brother, was afraid to say "No" to the people, and helped them.

But God was seeing everything, so He sent Moses back down the mountain.

When Moses got back to the camp, what he saw made him very angry. There was the large golden calf, with the Hebrews dancing to wild music and bowing down to the calf.

"What are you *doing?*" Moses shouted. "The living God rescued you from slavery and *this* is your gratitude to Him!"

When the people saw Moses, they trembled. "Look at his face! It glows! He has seen God," they cried.

In his fury Moses lifted the stone tablets over his head and smashed them on the ground. Then he shattered the golden calf, made a powder out of it, mixed it with water, and as punishment, forced the children of Israel to drink it.

Later on God told Moses and Aaron to bring two more stone tablets back up Mount Sinai. Then once again God etched the same commandments that He had written before.

After that Moses led the people once more on the long march into the wilderness toward the Promised Land.

Month after month, the people continued to distrust God and to disobey Him. Moses could not control them. Always they kept complaining, saying, "We want to go back to Egypt."

The Hebrews bowed before the golden calf

Finally, God's patience was exhausted. "None of you will ever enter the Promised Land. You will wander the rest of your days in the Wilderness. But I *will* lead your children into a beautiful land flowing with milk and honey.

"You, Moses, shall see the Promised Land with your own eyes, but you shall die on the edge of that land without entering it."

It happened just as God had said. For forty years the Hebrews wandered about in the desert. One by one, the men and women who had escaped from Egypt died. Only their sons and daughters were left alive.

One day when Moses was very old, he stopped his people by the banks of the Jordan River. Then slowly he climbed nearby Mount Nebo, which overlooked the river. On the other side was a lush green land dotted with wildflowers of every color. Wheat fields swayed in the wind like seas of gold. Looking at this beautiful land, Moses wept.

At last they had reached the Promised Land that God had promised to these descendants of Abraham, Isaac, and Jacob.

And there, in sight of his goal, Moses, one of God's great men, died.

It was the young man Joshua whom God chose to lead the people in Moses' place.

Soon Joshua led the entire caravan of Hebrews across the river Jordan. The sun shone golden above them as the carts and donkeys and children splashed through the water. Birds with red and blue and green plumes sang in the branches as they reached the banks of the Promised Land.

At last they were home.

A SHEPHERD BOY FIGHTS A GIANT

I Samuel 17:1–54

The Promised Land flourished under the hard work of the Hebrew people. Olive orchards spread across the green hills. Farms and vineyards dotted the land. Many children were born each year. Israel became a large nation.

But the Hebrews were not the only nation in this land. There were cruel tribes nearby—the Hittites, the Ammonites, and others who worshipped false gods and sacrificed their own children to golden idols. They were fierce people who loved to fight.

One of the tribes that often fought the army of Israel was the Philistines. Battle followed battle, and often the Hebrews lost.

Now God had a very special plan for one of His people, the young man David. He was still only a teenager, red-haired, with beautiful eyes and a handsome body. While his older brothers served in Israel's army, David, being the youngest, stayed home and guarded his father's sheep. Often when alone he played his wooden harp and made up songs of praise that he sang to God under the starry night skies.

The harvest was plentiful

David guarded his father's sheep

One day David's father, Jesse, told him that the Philistine army had gathered to fight Israel again.

In the Philistine army was a huge giant named Goliath, nearly ten feet tall. He frightened everyone. His spear was many yards long, and he protected himself with a shield of solid brass. Over his body he wore a coat of bronze.

Goliath had killed so many Hebrew soldiers that they lived in terror of him.

The army of Israel was camped on a flat plain one day when the Philistines came from the hills to challenge them. Goliath himself stood before them, towering like a huge tree.

"Come on! Fight me, if you dare," his voice trumpeted. If your best soldier can kill me, then we'll leave you alone. If not, that proves your God doesn't even exist. And the whole land will be ours."

That day David's father had sent him to carry a message to his brothers. David reached the army encampment just in time to see Goliath and to hear his bragging challenge. . . "Is your God afraid of Me? Can He find no one to defend His honor?" Goliath taunted. Then he withdrew to wait.

David looked around to see how many soldiers were coming forward, willing to fight the giant. But there was no one. Even Israel's commanders were afraid.

"We can't let a heathen giant say such awful things about our God," David thought. "Why is everyone so afraid?"

He stood there, remembering all the lions and bears he had killed when they had come to carry off a sheep from his father's flock. Constant practice with his slingshot had given David a fearsome aim: a zinging stone sinking deep between the wild animal's eyes or in its heart would topple it every time.

So David stepped forward. "I'll fight Goliath," he said.

The soldiers laughed at him. "You? You're only a boy. Goliath will squash you with one foot."

But David picked up three stones and put them into his leather

The army of Israel fought the Philistines

shepherd's pouch. Then he walked past the soldiers, past all the goatskin tents where others were hiding, out into the open space between the two armies.

"Here I am, Goliath," called David. "I have come to defend the Lord of Israel. And my God *is* with me."

Looking down at him, Goliath laughed. "What? The mighty Israel sends a small boy out to battle *me?* Why, I'll kill you like a grasshopper."

With that, he lifted his spear—as long as a tree trunk—and with a powerful thrust, hurled it at David.

A cry of fright went up from the Hebrew camp.

But David, quick on his feet, nimbly leapt aside. The spear missed him, bouncing harmlessly off a boulder.

Then, reaching into his shepherd's pouch, David drew out his sling and a stone. He placed the stone in the sling and began to swing it above his head.

"Now it's my turn," he shouted up at the giant. "I fight you in the name of the Lord God, and against Him you are powerless."

"Why, I'll kill you with my bare hands," Goliath growled. He lunged toward David with thundering steps.

David swung his sling faster and faster. The stone whistled through the air and sank deep into the Philistine's forehead. Goliath staggered and fell flat on his face without a whisper— unconscious.

Then David lifted Goliath's huge sword with both his hands and cut off his head.

The Philistine army fled.

David became a brave soldier. He led the soldiers of Israel into battle and drove out many of the cruel tribes from the land of Israel.

At the age of thirty, David was crowned King of Israel. After that he lived in a splendid palace in the city of Jerusalem.

The giant fell!

But in his heart David was still a shepherd boy who loved God's out-of-doors—the green pastures where the sheep and the fat baby lambs nibbled the green grass starred with flowers; the crystal-clear brooks; the shady canyons between the hills.

As King David sat in his richly furnished palace, thinking longingly of roaming free in God's beautiful world, he would write poems about it. Then when the people gathered to worship God, David would play his harp and sing his poems honoring the Lord. David's poems are in our Bible in what we call *The Psalms*.

One of David's songs tells us about his shepherd days. In Psalm 23 David tells us that Jesus wants to be our Shepherd to take care of us just as David had protected his family's sheep. . . The Lord is my Shepherd; He will see that all my needs are met.

He maketh me to lie down in green pastures;
He leadeth me beside the still waters.
　　Whatever my soul needs, He restores to me:
He leadeth me only in good and right paths
　　　that glorify Him.
Even though I have to walk through the valley of the shadow
　　　　　of death,
　　I will not be afraid:
because I know that You, Lord, art with me;
　　Your Shepherd's rod and staff are always there
　　　　to comfort me.
You, Lord, even prepare a banquet of celebration for me
　　for all my enemies to see;
You anoint my head with oil to bless me;
　　You not only fill my cup, it runs over.
I know that Your goodness and Your mercy will follow me
　　all the days of my life:
and when I am finished with my earth-life, I will dwell
　　in the house of the Lord with You forever.*

* This is a paraphrase for children of Psalm 23 in the King James Version.

100

Though David sinned and made many mistakes as a king, he always loved the Lord and sought His forgiveness. And God forgave David and blessed him, saying, "David is My beloved friend. He is a man after My own heart."

THE WISEST MAN

I Kings 3:4-14; I Chron. 22:6-10; I Kings 3:16-28; 6:1-37

When King David grew old, he passed on the crown of Israel to his son, Solomon. And then God appeared to Solomon in a dream.

"Solomon, now that you are king, tell Me, what shall I give you?"

Now Solomon was still a young man, and he might have asked for many selfish things. Instead of that, his first thought was of the people he had to govern. How could he be a good king over so many?

"Oh Lord," was the young king's answer, "I ask of You wisdom, that I may be able to discern between good and evil."

God was pleased with Solomon's answer. "Because you have asked for wisdom instead of wealth or power or a long life, I will give you all of these. You shall have a heart so wise and so understanding that there will have been none like you before your time nor after."

While Solomon was still a young man, David had summoned him to say, "My son, the Hebrew people have worshipped in a tent long enough. The Lord's request is that you build a temple to glorify God. If you do this, God shall be with you always."

So Solomon began building a temple atop Mount Moriah in Jerusalem. He saw to it himself that the silversmiths, wood-carvers, stone cutters, and sculptors followed the exact instructions God had given to his father, David. The work took seven years.

When at last it was complete, the entire nation of Israel gathered in Jerusalem to see their glorious temple. Like a rare jewel, it gleamed on the mountain of the Lord. The altar and all the trimmings were of solid gold. The curtains were sewn from purple, crimson, and violet cloth.

Last of all the people watched the priests carry into the temple the ark of God containing the two stone tablets with the ten commandments given to Moses. At that moment the pillar of cloud that had led the Hebrews from Egypt through the wilderness filled the place. By that the people knew that God was really with them. So brilliant was His glory that the priests who were serving there had to shield their eyes.

But even in the midst of the glory, the Lord gave Solomon a stern warning. "If you continue to obey Me, the royal line of your family will go on. But if you begin to worship other gods, the kingdom will be torn from your family. I will allow the temple to be destroyed, and the glory of Israel will fade."

So Israel was the splendor of the whole earth for many years. The brilliant white light of God's presence remained in that secret place of the temple, the "Holy of Holies."

As God had promised, Solomon became a king of astonishing wisdom.

One day two women came to Solomon's royal court. They climbed the steps to his throne, which was guarded by twelve golden lions. One of them held a sleeping baby.

The first woman cried, "Oh wise king, this woman has stolen my child, and now she claims that he belongs to her."

The second woman chimed in, "Oh wise and good king, this woman is lying. The child is mine, and she stole him from my arms while I was sleeping."

Solomon thought a moment, then hit upon a plan. "Give me your sword," he said to a palace guard. "I will divide the child in two and give half to each woman."

The first woman nodded. "If that's your decision, go ahead and cut him in two. If I can't have him, at least she won't have him either."

The second woman fell to her knees. "Oh please, sir, do not kill the child. I will give him up rather than see him die."

Solomon replied, "Give the baby to the second woman. She truly loves him and is obviously the real mother."

As Solomon's reputation spread, people came from everywhere to sit at his feet, to ask him questions, and get his advice. The Queen of Sheba traveled for three months from a far land to seek from Solomon the secrets of being a wise and just ruler.

He left some of his wisdom to us in three thousand proverbs (the *Book of Proverbs* in our Bible), each one a wise thought for good living.

As for the king's wealth, who could have measured it? Every day a caravan arrived at Solomon's palace from the kings of the east, who sent sparkling gems and treasure. Gold and silver became as common in his palace as pebbles in the streets of Jerusalem. The king owned fourteen hundred chariots and twelve thousand horses.

Like David, his father, Solomon had faults. The worst was that he began to worship other gods. This was the beginning of deep trouble for the nation of Israel.

After Solomon's death, Rehoboam, his son, reigned so unwisely that the kingdom split into two parts, with the people of the north, Israel, fighting the people of the south, Judah.

The heathen kings in surrounding lands watched like hungry wolves as the Hebrew people turned away from God and the strength of Israel crumbled. Secretly, they gathered their horses and chariots. They plotted, waiting for the right moment to attack Israel and carry the Hebrews into slavery once again.

The temple gleamed like a rare jewel

The Queen of Sheba arrives with her caravan of elephants

IN THE LIONS' DEN

Daniel 1; 2; 6; Ezra 1; 2; Micah 5:1–4

A very sad thing happened to the people of Israel. Because they turned away from God and worshiped false gods, the Lord removed His blessing and protection from them.

This gave Nebuchadnezzar, king of Babylon, a great opportunity. He gathered his horsemen, armed soldiers, and chariots, and they swept over the hills and fields of Israel, swinging their deadly swords. Many Hebrews were killed. The invaders took the golden treasures from the temple of Israel and then burned it. Then the cruel Babylonians led away the survivors—men, women, and children—in iron chains.

One of the captives led along the hot, dusty roads was a young Hebrew named Daniel. Unlike most of the people of Israel, Daniel remained faithful to God. When the Hebrew prisoners reached Babylon, King Nebuchadnezzar chose the best-looking and healthiest young men among them to live and study in his court. Daniel was one of those chosen.

In the court of Babylon, the young men were dressed in the best clothes and treated to the finest food in the land. They studied literature, languages, music, and other subjects as the king commanded them.

But Daniel would not eat any of the Babylonian food that had been offered to pagan idols. Instead, he ate simply, studied hard, and prayed daily for God's help and protection.

King Nebuchadnezzar awoke one morning in his bed of silk and goosedown, very upset. His eyes were bleary because a dream had troubled his sleep all night long. Yet in the morning light he could not remember his dream.

Summoning his wise men, he commanded them to tell him the dream and what it meant. They only shrugged. "How can we tell you what it meant when you don't even remember the dream?"

One of the men said, "We could ask that Hebrew, Daniel. He seems to know a lot about dreams and what they mean."

So Daniel was brought before King Nebuchadnezzar. He was prepared. He had been praying in his own room and God had already shown him the king's dream.

Now outside the city the king had erected a very tall statue of himself made of gold. He had ordered everyone to bow before the statue and worship him, the king, as a god. Daniel knew that King Nebuchadnezzar's dream was about this statue. . .

"In your dream, O King," Daniel told him, "you saw a huge statue in the form of a man. The head was made of the finest gold, the chest and arms were silver, the belly and thighs were bronze, the legs were iron, and the feet were part iron, part clay. A stone cut without human hands from a mountain fell on the statue's feet and crushed them.

The king on his golden throne was leaning forward, an excited look on his face. "Yes, yes! That was my dream. Now I *do* remember. Go on—"

"The God who rules heaven and earth wants to show you through a dream what will happen in the future," Daniel told the king. "The meaning is this—Your kingdom, Nebuchadnezzar, is powerful and splendid like gold. After you, other kings will arise whose kingdoms are less and less great, like silver, bronze, iron, and clay.

"And the stone that fell on the feet of the statue is a mighty King whom God will send to earth. His kingdom will be the greatest of all. It will reach to the ends of the earth."

King Nebuchadnezzar was impressed with Daniel. He knew that this Hebrew had some source of wisdom that his own wise men did not have. So that very day he made Daniel a ruler over the province of Babylon and head of all the wise men.

Naturally, the Babylonians were jealous of this foreigner. They kept trying to think of a way to get rid of Daniel.

King Nebuchadnezzar died and Darius mounted the throne. Daniel was a trusted friend of this new king too. Even so, the wise men thought of a way to trick Darius and get Daniel out of the way.

One morning a big group of them came before the throne. "King Darius, live forever. We're here to make a suggestion. Why don't you decree a royal law and make it very binding: 'Whoever shall ask a request of any god or man for thirty days, except of you, O King, that man shall be cast into a den of lions.' "

Without thinking and because this law seemed flattering to him, the king agreed.

Daniel heard about the new law, of course, yet went right on kneeling and praying to his God every day.

The wise men then caught him in the act of praying one day and went back to report to King Darius.

"Daniel has broken your new law," they told the king. "He prays alone to his God. So let him be cast into the den of lions. You have spoken, O King. Your word is law and cannot be broken."

Darius knew that his men had tricked him. He was stricken in heart. He had condemned to death his own friend.

Guards took Daniel to the mouth of a deep cave filled with hungry lions. They pushed him in, and began to roll a heavy boulder over the opening.

King Darius was there, very upset. He called down into the damp darkness of the cave, "Your God will save you, Daniel." And when the stone was set in place, Darius went and shut himself in his palace. All night long he went without food and sleep as he worried about Daniel.

The lions surrounded Daniel with claws sharp as daggers

In the dim light of the cave, Daniel sat on the jagged rocks. All around him, huge green eyes gleamed and fangs glistened. Back and forth the lions paced, with claws sharp as daggers, ready to spring.

But God sent an angel to shut the mouth of every lion, so that they would not harm Daniel.

In the morning Darius hurried to the cave with his guards and officials. The wicked wise men smiled to each other, expecting to find nothing left but a few bones.

But when the guards rolled the stone away, Daniel called up to them, "I'm fine. Quite safe. My God has delivered me."

Daniel was lifted from the cave on a rope. Darius angrily turned to his wise men. "You accused Daniel falsely and tricked me. Now *you* must die," he ordered.

They were thrown into the cave. And the hungry lions pounced upon them, tore their bodies apart, and fed upon them.

In time another king took the throne of Babylon. He set the Hebrews free and sent them back to the land of Israel. Dancing and singing, they returned to their home. The temple of God was rebuilt in Jerusalem, and the heathen tribes who had moved into the land were once again driven out.

Daniel and the other prophets continued to speak God's messages to the people. They told of the Heavenly King about whom Daniel had spoken to King Nebuchadnezzar.

"He will be called the Son of Man, and His kingdom will be filled with people from every nation and language. His throne will last forever," Daniel declared.

And the prophet Micah said, "He will be born in Bethlehem, although His true beginning was ages ago. He will lead His people like a Shepherd. And He will bring peace to the ends of the earth."

A false god

THE NEW TESTAMENT

THE NIGHT VISITOR

Luke 1:26–37; Matthew 1:18–25

It happened in a village called Nazareth, set in the hill country of Galilee. Traders, merchants, and soldiers sometimes passed through, bringing exciting news. But most of the time Nazareth was a quiet little town.

So the village was abuzz with excitement when Joseph, the carpenter, announced that Mary would soon be his wife. The men readied their musical instruments. Women began planning the wedding feast. At the village well, the girls set down their buckets and talked eagerly about the coming celebration.

Now Mary lived in a small, humble house on a terrace splashed with sun. This house was so white that sometimes it looked almost blue.

Mary was known throughout Nazareth as a gentle, generous young woman who loved God and tried to serve Him. Joseph too was a godly man, especially known for being a good carpenter and for his honesty in business.

One night Mary lay on her mattress of straw. Outside, she could see the dark sky filled with blazing stars.

All at once, a pale light began to shine through her window. Brighter and brighter it grew until it seemed as if the morning sun were rising right on her windowsill. And at the very heart of the light, an angel appeared.

''Hail, O favored one, the Lord is with you,'' the angel greeted her.

Mary sat up in bed, frightened, stunned that God would speak to *her*.

''Don't be afraid, Mary. I am Gabriel. God has sent me with this message. He has chosen you for the greatest honor ever given to any woman. You will bear a Son. You shall call Him Jesus, which means 'Savior.' He will be called 'the Son of the Most High God.' God shall give Him the throne of His ancestor, King David, and of His kingdom there shall be no end.''

Nazareth, hometown of Mary and Joseph   *The Angel Gabriel appeared to Mary*

Mary sat hugging her knees, trembling, trying to understand. "But how can I bear a child? I do not yet have a husband."

"Nothing is impossible with God," was Gabriel's reply. The Holy Spirit will fill you with the power of God, and the Child conceived in you will be called the Son of God."

Mary was filled with wonder. "I am God's handmaiden. Be it unto me according to your word."

And the angel disappeared.

For a time, Mary told no one of the angel Gabriel's visit, not even Joseph. She was not sure that anyone would believe her.

But after a time, when Mary felt the baby moving within her, she knew that she must tell Joseph. She hoped that he would receive this as happy news.

The day that Mary stood in the dusty carpentry shop and told Joseph her story, he looked puzzled, saying little.

That night Joseph tossed about restlessly on his bed. He felt that he must make an unhappy decision. If Mary had a baby with no husband, she would be disgraced in the village and he would be made fun of. Should not the engagement be broken and Mary sent to a distant relative?

As Joseph fell asleep, his dreams were filled with bright wings. The angel Gabriel appeared to him in a shining light and spoke.

"Joseph, son of David, do not send Mary away. She has done nothing wrong. The child within her is indeed the Son of God, conceived by the Holy Spirit. It is happening just as the prophet of old predicted:

A virgin will conceive and bear a son.
And the people will say, 'God is with us.' "

When Joseph awoke, the first fingers of sunlight were creeping up the sky. A smile spread across his face like the morning light. Now he knew that Mary's story was really true.

Mother and son

Everyone wants to see the new baby

And so Joseph took Mary to be his wife. She lived with him in a quiet home beside the carpentry shop, and they kept their secret in their hearts and treasured it.

A KING IS BORN

Luke 2:1–20

When Mary and Joseph were married, Israel was under the rule of the Roman Emperor, Caesar Augustus. His soldiers were posted everywhere, always tramping through the land, enforcing his cruel orders.

As the time drew near for Mary's baby to be born, the Emperor decided to take a census to see how many people were living in his huge empire. For this, every person in Israel had to travel back to his own hometown.

Joseph's hometown was Bethlehem. So one day Joseph helped Mary mount a donkey and led her out of Nazareth toward Bethlehem.

For many days Joseph led the shaggy donkey over dusty, hilly roads. By the time they reached Bethlehem late one evening, Mary's baby was about to be born.

Quickly Joseph went first to one village inn, then another. But all the innkeepers turned Joseph away, saying, "We're filled up. There's no place for you and your wife."

Mary was in great pain by this time and Joseph was desperate. Carefully he led the donkey around behind one of the inns, looking for shelter in the stable from the cold night.

As they entered, Joseph's lantern cast a dim light through the stalls and rafters. Sheep nuzzled their lambs. Doves cooed in their feathery nests. The old cow looked at them with her deep brown eyes and moved aside to share her straw bedding with Mary.

Mary and Joseph ride into Bethlehem

Thus it was that only the beasts in the stable heard the first small cry as the King of Heaven was born.

Joseph then placed the baby in Mary's arms. Tenderly, she wrapped Him in the swaddling clothes she had sewn for Him.

Out on the nearby hills shepherds had been grazing their flocks. Wrapped in their long cloaks to keep warm that night, they were sitting around a fire; one of them playing the flute.

Suddenly, their sleepy eyes were dazzled by a glistening light. In the column of radiance stood an angel of the Lord. The shepherds trembled in terror.

"Fear not," the angel announced, "I bring you good news! Here in the City of David, the Savior is born. He is Christ, the Lord. You will find Him wrapped in swaddling clothes, lying in a manger."

Suddenly, the night rang with joyful song. The sky was filled with a host of heavenly angels, drenching the very stars with melodious praise.

"Glory to God in the Highest!" they chorused. "Peace on earth, good will to men!"

The shepherds put out their fire and ran, stumbling, over the hills to Bethlehem. Some carried torches, others took newborn lambs as a gift for the King.

Breathless, they reached the stable and peered inside. There sat Joseph resting amid the animals, and Mary was humming a soft cradle song.

Wide-eyed and staring, the shepherds crept into the stable. "Hush, the child is sleeping!" they whispered to one another.

And to Mary and Joseph they said, "We have come to worship our newborn King!"

"We have come with gifts," said the wise men

The star led many people to Bethlehem

FOLLOWING A WANDERING STAR

Matthew 2

In a far eastern country, there were three wise, rich, and powerful kings. One night they noticed a mysterious star moving through the still darkness of the night sky. As they gazed at it, each felt a beckoning in his heart.

"Ancient wise men wrote of such a star," they reminded one another. "We must follow the star, for the prophecy has always been that it will lead to the great King sent from God Himself."

Together, the three Wise Men travelled over the night roads, led by the star. Moonlight sparkled on their gold, silver, and purple-woven robes, and on their jewelled rings. The steady clop, clop of camel hooves filled the darkness.

They carried gifts worthy of a King—small chests of gold, myrrh, and frankincense—rare and costly spices.

Over mountain passes, high and cold, they travelled, and through dry deserts. After many days and nights, the star led them into the land of Israel.

The three Wise Kings went straight to Jerusalem to the palace of Herod, who had the title of king over little Judea. Eagerly, they asked, "Where is the newborn King of the Jews? We have followed His star from the east, and have come to worship Him."

Herod was an evil king. Willingly, he obeyed all the harsh commands of the Roman emperor just so he would not lose his throne. But now he was frightened. Had someone appeared to take away his crown?

So he thought of a sly plan. "Our ancient prophets said this King would be born in Bethlehem. When you find Him, tell me where He is so that I may send a gift too."

But to his counselors he whispered, "Let the Wise Men find Him, then I'll kill the child."

The three kings urged their camels on toward Bethelem. The mysterious star moved on before them, low on the horizon. At last it stopped, gleaming brilliantly above a weathered stable.

The soldiers carried out Herod's terrible orders

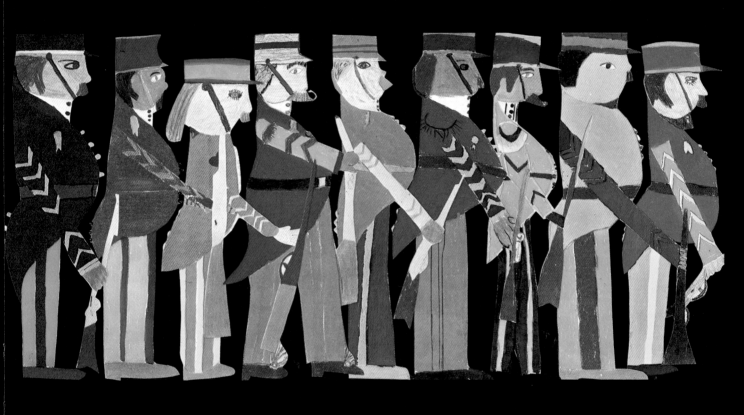

Entering, the kings saw Joseph and Mary, just as the shepherds had found them. And there, curled in his bed of straw, was the sleeping Christ Child.

Weeping for joy, the kings knelt in the straw before the newborn Baby, offering Him the presents they had brought.

That night, God spoke to the kings as they slept beside their camels. "Do not tell Herod where to find the Child, for great evil has filled his heart."

So the kings returned to their own lands by another route, and did not go back to Jerusalem.

Herod's face twisted in rage when he learned that he had been tricked. "Send my soldiers to Bethlehem," he shouted. "Kill every male child up to two years of age."

But as the soldiers headed for Bethlehem to carry out the king's cruel order, an angel spoke to Joseph in a dream. "Be quick, Joseph! Herod is looking for the Child to put Him to death. Get up and flee to Egypt."

Joseph obeyed. Before daybreak, he wrapped Mary and Jesus warmly and set them on the donkey. Quietly, they crept out of Bethlehem and fled to Egypt as the first rosy light of dawn colored the hills.

Only after Herod's death did Joseph return to Israel, where he settled down in Nazareth with Mary and the infant Jesus.

THE MISSING BOY

Luke 2:41–52

We do not know a great deal about Jesus as a boy. He lived in a home where He was taught to love and obey God. Like any normal boy He played with other village children and worked

The boy Jesus amazed the scholars

beside Joseph in the carpentry shop. His quick searching mind soon picked up his father's skills.

When Jesus was twelve, His family made the seventy mile trip to Jerusalem for the feast of the Passover. Jesus was with them to take part in the important yearly celebration.

There were so many people in the group returning to Nazareth that Joseph and Mary had been on the road many hours before they noticed that Jesus was not with them. Mary became very worried.

"Did you not see my Jesus?" she asked everyone.

But no one knew where Jesus was.

Greatly distressed, Joseph and Mary went all the way back to Jerusalem. For many hours they searched for Him.

Finally they found Him sitting in the Temple among the priests and scholars. These wise and experienced men had been astonished by Jesus' wisdom, by the penetrating questions He had asked, and by a knowledge far beyond His years.

Mary hugged Him joyfully, then softly scolded Him: "Oh, my Child, why did You do this to us?"

But Jesus only replied, "I'm sorry to have caused you worry. But it is time that I be about My Father's business."

As Jesus dutifully returned home with them, Joseph and Mary kept pondering that statement.

What was the destiny of their remarkable Son?

THE VOICE AND THE DOVE

Matthew 3:1–17; 4:1–11

As a young man, working with the tools and heavy wood in Joseph's carpentry shop, Jesus' muscles grew strong and hard.

Early every morning He would roam the green hills outside Nazareth, His appreciative eyes missing no detail. So often He was heard to comment, "Don't we have a beautiful world!"

The Holy Spirit descended upon Jesus

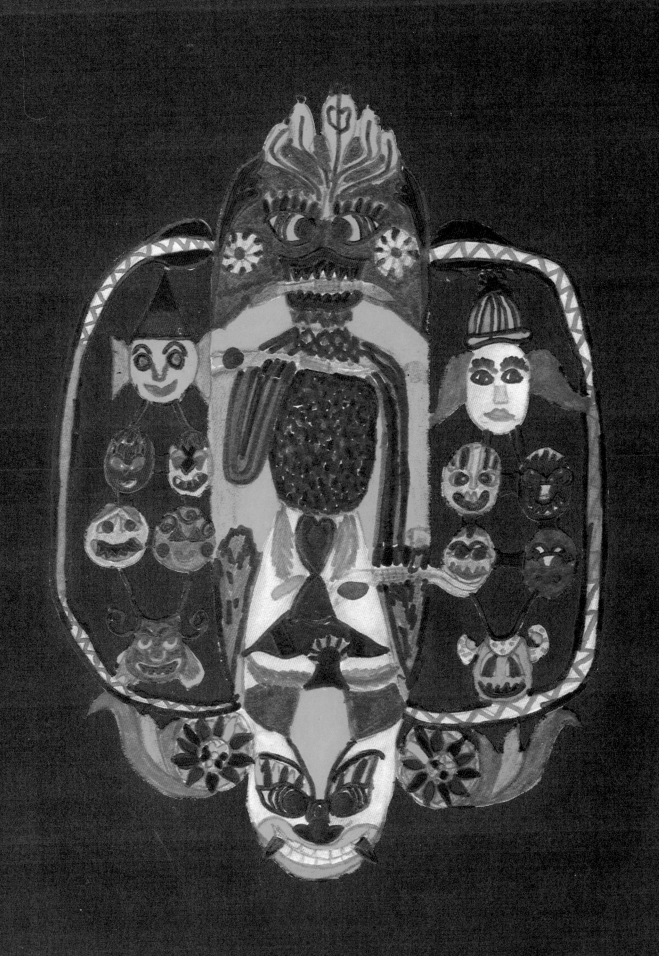

During these walks, as the sun warmed the grass, He would talk with His Heavenly Father. The love and wisdom He showed toward all His neighbors made Him a favorite in Nazareth. His was the kind of mind that quickly got to the heart of any question put to Him.

About the time Jesus reached manhood, a prophet of God named John the Baptist was preaching in the Judean wilderness. His home was a cave, and he ate locusts and wild honey. People came from Jerusalem and beyond to hear the message of this man who wore only a garment of coarse camel hair.

John's voice rang through the rocky valley and hills. "Prepare the way of the Lord!"

As they listened to John, many of the people would openly confess their sins, then be baptized in the flowing waters of the Jordan River. The hillsides and banks would be crowded with people watching.

One day, Jesus Himself stepped from the bank into the swirling waters. John's spirit leapt inside him when he saw Jesus.

"Behold, the Lamb of God," John called out to the crowds. "He will take away the sins of the world. Though I baptize you with water, He will baptize you with the Holy Ghost and with fire!"

When Jesus reached John in the middle of the river, John spoke to Him quietly. "I am not worthy even to carry Your shoes. Nor to baptize You. You should be baptizing me."

Jesus' quiet reply was, "My Father in heaven told Me to do this. We must obey whatever He asks."

The crowds on the riverbank watched as John baptized Jesus. As Jesus rose up from the water, the people were startled by the rushing sound of wings. Bright as a flash of lightning, the Holy Spirit descended upon Him, as gentle as a white dove.

A voice spoke from the sky. "This is my beloved Son. I love Him, and He always pleases me."

But not everyone there heard the Voice or saw the Dove, only those whose hearts were open to see.

Soon after that the Holy Spirit Himself led Jesus by a rugged path into the wilderness.

In the dry, barren hills Jesus prayed. For forty days and nights He ate nothing. During this time, Satan, the same evil one who had tempted Adam and Eve in the Garden of Eden, tried three times to make Jesus sin.

But each time Jesus resisted Satan, and finally the devil left Him.

After that the angels came from heaven to bring Him food and to comfort Him. In this way Jesus prepared Himself for the marvelous work He was about to begin.

Jesus was then thirty years old.

THE WEDDING PARTY
John 2:1–11

Not long after Jesus returned from the wilderness, He was invited to a wedding celebration in the village of Cana. Jesus' mother was there too, and a few of the disciples who had begun to travel with Him.

The wedding was a joyous event. Gifts were given. Laughter and music tumbled together as the musicians played.

Cups were filled and refilled as more and more people arrived. Then the head-servant drew the host aside. ''Sir, we've run out of wine. Some of your guests have had none.''

Wringing his hands, the host lamented, ''This is terrible. What *can* I do?''

Mary had overheard the poor man. Turning to Jesus, she whispered, ''These people are very embarrassed because they have no more wine.''

Jesus, perhaps thinking that it was too early for Him to perform miracles, answered in a low voice, ''My hour has not yet come.''

But Mary knew her Son well. She knew that He could not

Musicians played at the wedding feast

remain insensitive to any misfortune, big or small, happening to any of His friends. So she turned to the servants and said, "Do whatever my Son tells you."

And Jesus stood up and pointed to six stone jars that stood empty by the door. "Fill each jar to the brim with water," He told the servants.

The stone jars were large, and the servants carried many pails of water from the well to fill them.

Then Jesus said, "Dip a cup into one of the jars and take it to the host."

One of the servants took a cup, and as he dipped it in the jar, the water turned deep ruby red. Then he carried the cup to the host.

The host took one sip and, astonished, called to the groom, "This is the best wine we've had all day. Usually, the finest wine is served first. How wonderful that you have saved the very best wine for the last!"

But the servants and the disciples who had come with Jesus knew the truth. They were awed. Truly, here was a Man with extraordinary power.

This was the first miracle that Jesus performed.

THE HAPPIEST PEOPLE
Matthew 10:1–4; 5; 6

By now Jesus had chosen twelve men to be His friends and companions. They were called apostles, or disciples, and there were twelve in all: Peter, Andrew, James, John, Matthew, Philip, Bartholomew, Thomas, Simon, Thaddaeus, another man also named James, and Judas. Many others followed Jesus, but these men were closest to Him.

At first the twelve disciples did not know that Jesus had come from heaven; they thought that He was only a good teacher.

With Him they walked the dusty roads from village to village. Everywhere Jesus went, the disciples heard Him teaching people about a loving God who is like a Father, and about the kingdom of heaven—not up in the sky, but right here on earth.

In those days some of the religious leaders were very stern and proud. They were called Pharisees. They set up their own rules about how to serve God. If one of their people broke even the smallest rule, he was punished harshly.

Jesus' teaching was different from that of the Pharisees. His words fell like clear water on thirsty hearts. People smiled and laughed for joy when He spoke. Everywhere, word spread about this amazing young Teacher who was filled with such love and wisdom, yes—and even the power to make sick people well.

One day Jesus climbed up on a mountainside and sat down to talk to the people as they gathered about Him on the cool green grass:

"Happy are the poor in spirit, for the kingdom of heaven belongs to them.

"Those who mourn will be comforted. And they will be filled with God's heavenly joy.

"Happy are those who do not use strength or violence to get their way. The whole earth will be given to them.

"Happy are those who long for goodness as if it were food and water. They shall be filled.

"Happy are the merciful; mercy will be shown to them.

"Happy are the pure in heart, for they will see God face to face.

"Happy are the peacemakers. Everyone will know them as the children of God.

"Happy are those who are taunted and treated badly

because they follow God's ways. The kingdom of heaven belongs to them.

"Be happy when men mistreat you or tell lies about you for following Me. Be full of joy, because you have a rich reward awaiting you in heaven."

The mountainside was silent, except for the sighing of the wind and the singing of birds.

"In the Old Book of the Law," Jesus went on, "it says that if someone strikes you, you are to punch him back. But now I bring you a higher Law, the Law of love. So I say to you, do not love only those who love you; you must love your enemies too. Forgive your enemies and do good to those who wrong you."

Some of the Pharisees who had come to spy on Jesus were seated in the grassy meadow too. They did not like this talk about the Law of love. It made no sense to them.

Jesus saw them and knew what was in their hearts. "Some people love to show how religious they are," He dared to say. "They brag about their good deeds in public, and they stand on street corners praying loudly. By doing this, they hope that men will praise them and think they are holy.

"But I say, do your good deeds quietly, not to be seen of men. God sees you. Pray to God when you are alone. He hears you."

A man seated near Jesus asked, "Lord, will You teach us how to pray?"

Jesus thought a moment, then said, "Pray like this:

Our Father which art in heaven, Hallowed be thy name. They kingdom come. Thy will be done on earth, as it is in heaven. Give us this day our daily bread. And forgive us our debts, as we forgive our debtors. And lead us not into temptation, but deliver us from evil: For thine is the kingdom, and the power, and the glory, for ever. Amen."

Happy are the people of God

When Jesus had finished, the people were smiling, with tears of happiness in their eyes. The Pharisees had always taught that God was stern and far off; here was Jesus calling Him "Father!"

But one of the Pharisees spoke out angrily. "How dare you call God 'Father'?"

Jesus said, "Because God *is* your Father. That is why you should always talk to Him in prayer. Tell Him all your needs, and never worry about anything."

He pointed to a tree nearby. Chirping, singing birds flitted about in the shady branches.

"Look at the birds of the air," He said. "They never harvest grain or struggle to store up their food in barns. And yet God feeds them. So if God feeds even the birds, will He not see to *your* needs too?

"So do not worry, saying, 'What if I have no food?' Or even 'What if I have no home?' Seek with all your hearts to live in God's kingdom, and He will take care of all your needs."

The crowd on the mountainside had never heard such good news. With every word that Jesus spoke, the people could feel heavy burdens being lifted from their hearts.

But the Pharisees went back to Jerusalem, speaking against Jesus. . . . "How dare this man teach about God," they grumbled. "He's just a carpenter. He's never even studied in our schools."

What really bothered the Pharisees was that if the people turned to Jesus for help, then they would turn away from them and their teachings. But the more the Pharisees talked against Jesus, the larger grew the joyful crowds that followed Him each day.

ONE WITHERED HAND

Luke 6:6–11

As Jesus told everyone about the kingdom of God coming to earth *now,* it was like a warm light spreading across the land. For those who let the light shine in their heart, things began to

His hand was healed!

change. Masters stopped beating their servants. Servants no longer stole from their masters. Men forgave each other, and settled their bitter arguments. Women stopped gossiping about their neighbors.

Satan was angry when he saw all this. God had thrown Satan out of heaven ages ago when he had tried to steal God's throne. Since then, Satan had wandered to and fro over the earth, causing wars, sickness, and crimes. Somehow, he knew, he must stop Jesus.

One Sabbath day Jesus went to worship in the synagogue in Capernaum. Many of the Pharisees were there, dressed in fine robes, praying aloud for all to hear.

A man walked in whose arm was twisted, his hand withered. He saw Jesus and rushed toward Him.

"Please, Master, will You heal my hand?" he begged.

Now the Pharisees did not allow anyone to work on the Sabbath. This was one of their strictest rules. No one could even carry a bucket of water.

Jesus knew they were watching and that the Pharisees would think of healing as "work." He turned and asked them, "Is it all right to do God's work on the Sabbath? Or should I allow this man's sickness to continue? Is life and health better? Or sickness and death?"

But the Pharisees refused to answer.

So Jesus said to the man, "Stretch out your hand."

As the man slowly opened his withered hand, it stopped trembling and became strong like his other hand.

The Pharisees were so furious that they began spreading wicked lies: "Jesus has power over demons only because he is Satan himself," they told the people. "He even breaks the Sabbath law by healing people."

But the common people were excited about what Jesus was doing. What could be wrong with healing people?

Some said, "Perhaps He has come to drive the Romans out of our land."

Demons came out of the man

And others added, "Yes, He must be the Savior, the One God always promised to send to save Israel."

STORM AT SEA

Mark 4:35–41

One day Jesus and His disciples decided to sail across the Sea of Galilee. The breeze unfurled the sails and carried their boat out over the calm, sunny waters.

Jesus was tired from their travels. He stretched out on a cushion and fell sound asleep, leaving His disciples to row.

While He slept, the sky grew dark with black clouds. A rising wind howled through the sails. Waves kept splashing over the bow, and the boat began to sink.

Jesus' disciples shook Him. "Master, wake up! *Save* us. Don't You *care* if we drown?"

Slowly Jesus sat up, rubbing His eyes. His men were huddled together in the pitching boat, their eyes wide with terror.

Rising, He grasped the gunwales to steady Himself. Facing into the storm, His voice rang out, "Wind, I rebuke you. Enough of this!" Then to the sea, "Peace! Be still."

The wind caught its breath and stopped moaning. The rising peaks of water began to settle down until at last they were as still as glass.

Then Jesus turned to His friends. "Why were you so afraid?" He asked them. "Is your faith in God *still* so small?"

Whereupon He sat down to rest again just as if nothing had happened.

Above the open boat, the sky was clearing. The twelve men whispered among themselves. "What kind of Man is this? Even the wind and the sea obey Him!"

THE HEALING TOUCH

Luke 5:1–16; 8:41–56

One day Jesus and the twelve met a man out on a lonely road. His friends had driven him out of town because he had an illness called leprosy. Horrible to look at, they called it "unclean," and were afraid of catching it.

So the poor man limped along, leaning on a staff. Sores covered him from head to toe. His feet were wrapped in heavy, tight bandages.

When the leper saw Jesus and the twelve walking toward him, he thought they too would drive him away. Instead, Jesus walked nearer and nearer, for He was not afraid of any disease. Seeing pity on Jesus' face, the leper knelt before Him beseechingly, "Lord, if You will, You can make me clean."

Jesus reached out and lovingly placed his hand on the sick man's scarred forehead. "Of course, I will. Be clean!" He commanded.

At once, the sores began to disappear. The blush of good health returned to the sick man's cheeks.

"I'm whole again!" the man laughed and shouted. He threw down his staff, began to leap up and down and dance. "Now I can go back home again!" he rejoiced. "Oh, thank You, Master. Thank You!"

And in every town the word spread. "Jesus heals the sick." It even spread back to Jesus' home town of Nazareth where most of the citizens remembered Joseph's son just as a godly, quiet young carpenter.

In Nazareth a wealthy ruler named Jairus lived in a large house surrounded by flowering gardens and olive groves. He was a ruler of the synagogue, and others in the town never decided any urgent matter without first coming to ask his opinion.

Most of all, Jairus was proud of his only child, a little daughter. She was a beautiful, happy child who loved to run and climb the olive or fig trees or skip through the fields.

One morning a servant ran to Jairus as he sat in council with the other leaders.

"Master," said the servant, "your daughter has a raging fever. She's very sick, sir. Your wife bids you hurry home."

Jairus rushed home and knelt at his daughter's bedside. Her hair was wet with fever. All day long the child tossed from side to side, first shivering, then hot and in pain.

The finest doctors were summoned. They tried every remedy they knew. Nothing they did seemed to help.

Early the next morning a servant came to Jairus again. "Master," he suggested, "when the women returned from the well this morning, they reported that the one called Jesus has returned to Nazareth. Everyone is saying that He can heal the sick. Do you think—?"

"Oh, *yes!* Great idea! I'll search Him out immediately."

So Jairus hurried out through the morning streets. He was delighted when he found Jesus walking through the market place with His twelve disciples.

Jairus fell on his knees before the Master. "Please, sir. My little girl is *so* sick. The physicians cannot help her. Would You, sir, come and heal her?"

Jesus lifted Jairus to his feet. "Of *course* I will come," was His gentle reply.

As they walked together, people crowded into the streets from every shop to see the Teacher. From the crowd, a hand slipped out and touched the hem of Jesus' cloak.

"Who touched Me?" Jesus asked, stopping in the street.

Jesus' disciples were astonished. "Why, the whole town is pressing around You, Master. Why would You ask which one touched You?"

Jesus insisted, "I felt healing power go out from Me."

An older woman, standing near Him, spoke up in a trembling voice. "For twelve years I've been bleeding from a terrible disease. But I knew I could be healed, if only I could touch the hem of Your garment."

Jesus smiled at her. "My daughter, don't be afraid. Be comforted. Your faith has made you well."

The woman's face brightened. She knew that her bleeding had already stopped. "I *am* well again," she exulted.

Jairus was overjoyed. Now he *knew* Jesus could heal his little girl. Eagerly, he urged Jesus and His apostles to hurry on through the crowd.

But before they reached Jairus' home, a man came running to meet them. He had been crying. "Sir, I have bad news," he blurted out. "Do not trouble the Master further. Your little girl is dead."

Before Jairus could say a word, Jesus grasped his shoulders, looking deep into his eyes. "Pay no attention to the message, Jairus. *Trust* Me. Just believe, and your little girl will be all right."

At Jairus' home, they found the courtyard already full of weeping, wailing neighbors. Musicians were playing a slow funeral dirge.

Jesus whispered to Jairus, "Send all these gloomy people away. Let us go to see your daughter."

After Jarius had cleared the house, Jesus would allow only His three apostles, Peter and James and John, along with the child's father and mother to go into her room with Him.

The little girl lay on her bed. The red flush of fever was gone from her face. She lay as quiet and still as marble.

Jesus touched her cold hand. Looking down at her tenderly, He said, "Rise up, little one."

At once, death flew from her like a black raven. She drew a sharp breath. Her eyelids fluttered open. Pink began to creep back into her cheeks.

Then she smiled up at her mother and father. "Daddy, where was I?—I feel much better now. But I'm *hungry*."

Jesus smiled. "Food for the little one," He directed.

Even as the food was being brought, Jairus and his wife kept hugging their little girl and thanking Jesus over and over for raising their little girl from the dead.

No wonder Jesus kept telling people, "You should no longer fear the darkness. *I am the light of the world.*"

And the people marvelled, saying, "Even death cannot stop this man."

Death flew from her like a black raven

WHY JESUS LOVED CHILDREN

Luke 9:46–48; 18:15–17

Every tongue in Israel now repeated some story about Jesus' miracles. The twelve disciples became very proud because they traveled with such a famous Teacher. They had even heard that some men wanted to make Jesus king of Israel.

One afternoon as they travelled down a sunny road, a few of the disciples began to argue. Simon was boasting, ''I will be the greatest in Jesus' kingdom since He always turns to me first.''

''Not so,'' young John interrupted. ''I am Jesus' closest friend. He's going to seat me at the right side of His throne. And my brother James will sit at His left.''

In a moment they were all arguing and shoving each other.

Jesus stopped them. ''Don't you understand why I have come? Haven't I taught you anything about the kingdom of heaven yet? You push and shove because you want to be first. But I tell you, in My kingdom the first shall be last, and the last shall be first.''

Still, the twelve men did not really understand what Jesus meant.

Later, Jesus sat down at the edge of a village to rest. Some young mothers came to Him. From behind their skirts, their little children peeked shyly at Jesus with great, round eyes.

''Will You bless our children, Master?'' one mother asked. But the disciples began to shoo them away.

Jesus silenced them. ''Let the little children come to Me,'' He said, beckoning to them.

Slowly, timidly, the little ones crept from behind their mothers' skirts. Then, with a scurry of bare feet, they surrounded Jesus, clinging to Him as He hugged them. Soon they were taking turns climbing into Jesus' lap and talking to him.

He stroked their hair, then blessed each one with His strong carpenter's hands.

He loved all the children

Later Jesus gathered His disciples around Him. "There's no way that you can enter the kingdom of heaven," He told them sadly, "unless you, all of you, become like these little children we saw today."

And the disciples were ashamed that they had become so proud.

FIVE THOUSAND HUNGRY PEOPLE
John 6:1–15

On another day Jesus stopped to pray in a rocky place, far from any of the towns. Still, a great number of people came in search of Him. They sat down on the hillside and pleaded, "Teach us more about the kingdom of heaven."

As the day grew longer, more and more kept coming. Finally, there were five thousand men, women, and children. By the time Jesus had finished teaching, it was late and everyone was very hungry.

The disciples were worried. "Master," they said, "these people have no food. There's no way to get any out here. Shouldn't we send them away before darkness?"

Jesus had noticed a little boy at the front of the crowd clutching a basket of woven reeds.

"What have you in your basket?" Jesus asked him.

The boy ran over, eagerly opening his basket. Inside were five loaves of barley bread and two small fishes. "It's my supper. But You may have it, Master," he offered, holding the basket up to Jesus.

Thanking the little boy, Jesus took the loaves and fishes and lifted them up toward heaven. Then He blessed them, and broke them into small pieces.

"Here," He said, handing the pieces to His disciples. "Now tell everyone to sit down in little groups. Then I want you to serve this food until everyone has eaten as much as he wants.''

Puzzled, the apostles looked at each other. How could the small bits of bread and fish in their hands feed such a big crowd? But Jesus had spoken in His no-nonsense voice, so finally they obeyed.

Thomas took his small share over to a widow with seven children.

''These hungry youngsters will devour every morsel I have,'' he thought.

Eagerly, each child broke off a piece of bread and some fish, then passed it along. Last, the mother tore off her portion. Strangely, she handed Thomas a larger piece of bread and more fish than he had started with.

''Thank you,'' she said, as Thomas stared in amazement. The bread was multiplying!

And so it went as the apostles walked up and down the crowded hillside, feeding all the men, women, and children. Everyone ate until they were full.

The disciples ate too, all that they wanted. Even the sparrows and blackbirds came to feast on the crumbs that were dropped.

When the scraps were gathered, twelve baskets were filled to overflowing with the leftover bread and fish. The disciples could scarcely believe their eyes.

After the crowd had gone, Jesus sat with His men around a crackling fire as the evening deepened into night. ''There's more to learn from what you saw this afternoon,'' He told them. ''*I am the bread of life.* My flesh is the *living* bread that has come down from heaven. My mission on earth is to give Myself to save the whole world.'' Then Jesus asked them, ''Who do you say I am?''

As the moon rose over the hills, they sat silent, not knowing how to answer.

Finally, Peter spoke up. ''I say that you are the Christ, the One God has chosen to save all of us from our sins.''

''At last, you know the truth,'' Jesus exclaimed. ''God Him-

self has revealed this to you."

Then He told them about the future, saying that He would soon go to Jerusalem where evil men would arrest Him and nail Him to a cross. They grew quiet and sad as He spoke.

"But you must remember this," said Jesus. "On the third day, I will rise from the dead."

As the apostles curled in their cloaks that night, they were wondering what all this could mean.

MIRACLE AT BETHANY

John 11:1–53; Matthew 20:22, 28

A home in Bethany, not far from Jerusalem, was one of Jesus' favorite stopping places. This was the home of Lazarus and of his sisters, Mary and Martha.

One day someone came to tell Jesus, "Come quickly, Lord. Your friend Lazarus is dangerously ill."

His disciples were surprised that instead of rushing to Bethany, their Master let two days go by.

Finally, He said to them, "It is time now to go to Bethany. Our friend Lazarus is dead. What is about to happen will increase your faith."

As Jesus and His disciples neared Bethany, a great crowd came to meet them. These were the mourners who had come to sympathize with Mary and Martha.

Out of the group Martha appeared and ran to kneel at Jesus' feet. "Lord," she sobbed, "if only You had been here, my brother Lazarus would not have died!"

"Lazarus will rise again," Jesus told her. "If a man has faith in Me, he shall come back to life. Do you believe this, Martha?"

But Martha was too upset to hear what Jesus was saying and she hurried off to get her sister Mary.

Soon Mary also was huddled before Jesus with the same hopeless words, "Oh, Lord, if You had just been here, our brother would not have died."

Since He loved this family so much, Jesus was soon mingling His tears with theirs. Then He asked, "Where is Lazarus? Where have you laid him?"

"Come and see, Lord. . ."

The crowd approached the tomb. It was a cave with a big stone over the opening.

Jesus requested, "Take the stone away."

"Lord," Martha said, "it has been four days since my brother died. His body will already be decaying."

Patiently, Jesus reminded her, "Did I not tell you, Martha, that if you would have faith, you would see the glory of God? So—let the stone be taken away!"

As some men rolled the stone back, Jesus lifted up His eyes and said, "Father, I thank You that You *always* hear Me." Then He cried with a loud voice, "Lazarus! Come forth!"

And Lazarus struggled forth, but still bound round and round with grave cloths.

"Loose him and let him go," Jesus ordered.

When Lazarus himself led the group back into town, never had there been such a celebration in Bethany.

Yet when the chief priests in Jerusalem heard of this great miracle, they were furious. "What tricks does He use?" they exclaimed. "We could explain the Jairus girl. She was obviously not dead, but in a coma, and Jesus brought her out of it. But the Lazarus trick is too much."

One of them, Caiphas, declared, "'If Jesus keeps this up, the people will have more faith in Him than in us. We can't let this go on."

So they decided. *Jesus of Nazareth must die. His power has become too great.*

At the same moment Jesus was saying to His disciples, "Can you drink the cup that I am going to drink? The Son of Man has come not to be served, but to serve, and to give His life as a ransom for many. . . ."

TRIUMPHANT RIDE ON A DONKEY

Mark 11:1–10

For almost three years Jesus travelled the land, healing the sick, comforting the hurting, teaching of God's love. One day as He rested on the Mount of Olives overlooking the city of Jerusalem, He directed His disciples, "Go into a nearby town. You will find a donkey tied to a rail on a street corner. Bring him back to me. If anyone stops you, just say, 'The Lord needs him.' "

So they went and found the donkey, just as Jesus had said, and led the donkey back to the Mount of Olives.

Jesus mounted the little beast and took the reins. "Come," He said, "it is time to enter Jerusalem."

As they passed through the stone archways into the city, people shouted from house to house, "Jesus is coming! Jesus is coming!"

Merchants ran from the market. Women left their laundry. Children stopped reciting their lessons and pushed aside their books.

As they saw Jesus approaching, people took off their cloaks and spread them over the dusty street. Young men climbed up trees and cut palm branches to make a carpet for Him to ride over.

The shouting echoed through the city. "Hosanna! Hosanna! Blessed is the One God has sent to save us! Hosanna in the highest!"

As the crowds along the streets cheered, the city officials were outraged.

"If the Romans see that the people want to make Jesus their king, they will send in more soldiers to destroy us. Then our business will be finished for good."

"Yes," said the Pharisees, "but we cannot touch Him or the people will rise against us. Perhaps we could find some friend of His to turn against Him." And they smiled wickedly.

One of the priests held up a bag. In it was thirty pieces of silver.

"We could offer this to the man who will betray Jesus. It shouldn't be too hard to find someone willing to betray an innocent man for thirty pieces of silver."

And they set out secretly to find the man.

Jerusalem welcomes Jesus with palm branches

THE LAST SUPPER

John 13:1–27

On the day of the Passover celebration, the streets were thronged with bustling shoppers. The holiday would begin at sundown, and people hurried to buy bread and candles and other needed supplies before the shops closed.

Judas Iscariot, one of the twelve apostles, also pushed his way in and out of the busy shops. Since he carried the money bag for Jesus and the others, he was always the one to buy what was needed.

One of the chief priests, seeing Judas, called him out of the crowd into an alleyway.

"I have seen you with Jesus," said the priest, and he opened his bag of silver for Judas to see. "The High Priest wants to see Jesus. But no one knows where he is staying in Jerusalem. This money is a reward for the man who will lead us to the Teacher tonight."

Judas stared at the gleaming silver as he talked to the priest. For three years, he had followed Jesus. It had not been an easy life. Many nights he had slept on cold, stony ground. Sometimes he and the others had had little to eat. Always they were jostled by people . . . people . . . people.

Satan also was watching Judas. He saw a black pit opening in Judas' heart. Like a dark wind, Satan entered into him.

"Yes," Judas said to the priest. "I'll come back tonight and lead you to Jesus. But now I must hurry back—or the others will wonder where I am."

That evening, at starlight, in a quiet upper room in Jerusalem, Jesus lit the Passover candles. Then He and the apostles sat down to their special meal of unleavened bread, bitter herbs, and wine.

When they had almost finished eating, Jesus lifted up a piece of bread. As they watched, He broke it.

"This is what will happen to My body," He told them quietly. "It will be broken for you. From now on, you will break bread like this to remind yourselves of Me." And He gave them the bread to eat.

Reaching out, He lifted up a cup of wine.

"This cup of wine is like My blood. God is making a new agreement with men. My blood is going to be shed for the sins of the whole world. Divide this cup among yourselves," He said. "Drink all of it."

And the cup was passed from hand to hand around the table.

As they drank, suddenly, Jesus made a startling statement. "One of you is going to betray Me."

The apostles looked at each other. "Is it I, Master?" each one asked.

Young John leaned close to Jesus and whispered, "Who is it, Lord?"

Jesus answered quietly, "I will hand this piece of bread to My betrayer."

He turned and looked Judas straight in the eye. Then He thrust the piece of bread into his hand. "Go quickly, and do what you must do," He said softly.

Judas stood up, looking frightened and angry all at once. The other apostles had not heard Jesus' remark to John. They thought Judas was going out to pay for their meal. Judas turned and left the room, the darkness in his heart as black as the shadows of the night outside.

BETRAYED

Luke 22:31–62

Peter got to his feet, standing straight and tall. "Master, even if everyone else turns from You, I will *never* leave You," he boasted.

But Jesus answered sadly, "I tell you, Peter, tomorrow morning, before the rooster crows, you will have denied three times that you ever knew Me."

Then Jesus led the apostles out into the hushed, moonless night. The streets were empty as they left Jerusalem and crossed the brook Kidron. Up a long trail they walked to the top of the Mount of Olives. There they entered a garden called Gethsemane, fragrant with flowers among the ancient olive trees.

"I must stop here and pray," Jesus told His apostles. "My heart is sad. Please stay by Me, if you will, tonight," He pleaded.

Jesus then walked on a little way ahead of them. At a bend in the path, He fell to His knees and began to pray.

There in the dark garden, under the twisted branches of the olive trees, Jesus shook with fear. Sweat poured down His face like great drops of blood.

"Father, I am terrified by what is about to happen to Me. It is like drinking a cup of the most bitter wine. How I wish it were possible for You to take this cup away from Me! Nevertheless, My will is not what's important. I will do exactly what *You* want Me to," Jesus prayed.

The night was silent except for the rustling of branches in the wind. Finally, Jesus rose from His knees and went back down the path to find the disciples. They were wrapped in their cloaks, propped against the trees, already asleep.

He shook them awake. "Could you not watch and pray with Me even for a little while?"

Two more times after going back to pray, He returned only to find the disciples dozing again. The third time He looked at them sadly. "Sleep on now," He said. "Take your rest. It is too late. My betrayer is at hand."

Just at that moment, the stillness was broken by distant voices and the sound of trampling feet coming up the path. Another moment and the disciples saw a group approaching—temple guards, carrying swords and torches. They were being led by Judas, of all people.

When they reached the edge of the garden, Judas came forward. The trees cast long shadows in the light from his torch. Like an old friend, he walked straight up to Jesus and kissed His cheek.

"Hello, Master," he smiled, cunningly.

"Judas, must you betray Me with a *kiss?*" Jesus asked quietly.

Immediately, the temple guards rushed to Jesus, roughly tying His hands as if He were a criminal.

Peter drew his sword and ran about swinging wildly. But Jesus told him, "Put down your weapon, Peter. Those who live by the sword will die by the sword."

Pushing and shoving, the guards led Jesus away.

In fright and confusion, the disciples fled, leaving their Master alone with His captors.

Jesus was dragged through the night streets to the palace of the High Priest.

All of the Pharisees and religious leaders were gathered in a large hall lit by torches to hold a mock trial. They had already paid some criminals to testify against Jesus. But the men got confused in their own lies, so that their stories made no sense.

Meanwhile, Peter had sneaked along the side streets, keeping out of the light, following the mob. He sat miserably in the palace courtyard, trying to warm himself by a sputtering fire. The first grey light of dawn was in the sky, and still he had heard no word about what was happening to Jesus.

A young girl who served the High Priest came out to add some sticks to the fire. She looked at Peter in the faint light and asked, "Aren't you one of Jesus' friends?"

Peter was suddenly terrified that he too would be arrested. "No, I don't know Him," he replied quickly.

"You must be a friend of His," the girl persisted. "I've seen you with Him in the hills many times."

"You're mistaken. I'm not one of His," Peter replied. And

The Garden of Gethsemane   *The soldiers arrested Jesus*

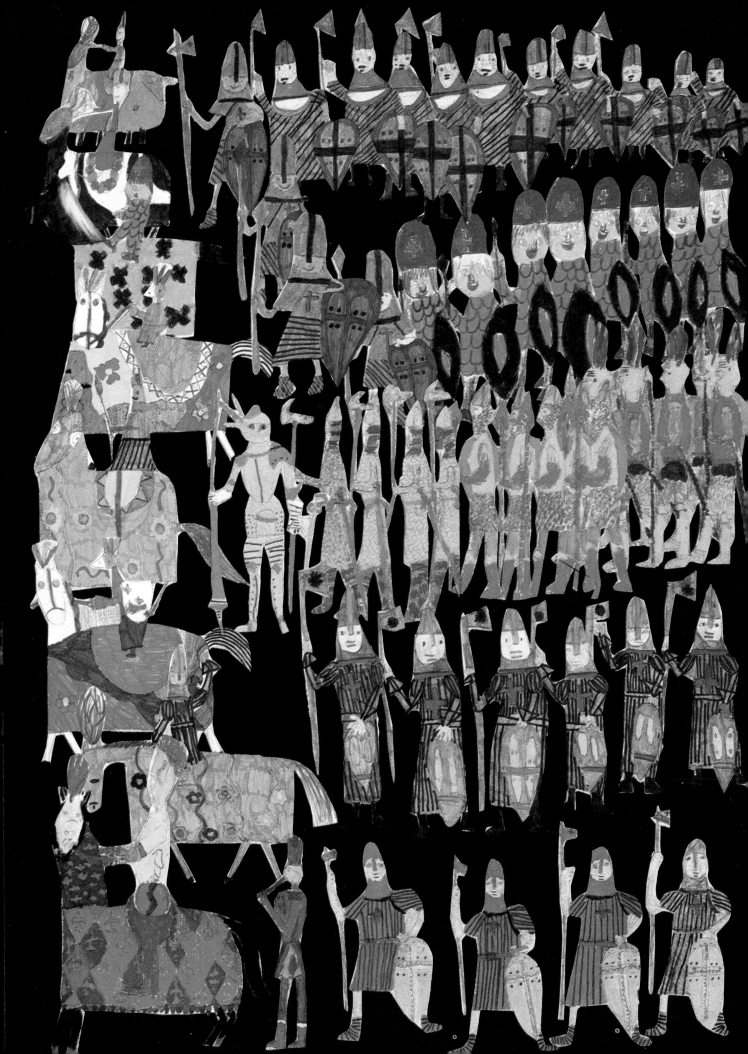

he pulled his cloak closer about his face.

Some other men were also sitting by the fire. They peered closely at Peter and said, "You *must* have been with Jesus. You speak with a Galilean accent, just the way He does."

"No!" shouted Peter. This time he let out some curses. "I don't even know who the Man is!"

The words had scarcely escaped his lips when Peter heard on the morning air the loud crowing of a rooster.

Then he remembered Jesus' words. So he, Peter, had denied His beloved Master three times, just as Jesus had said he would.

Peter went out into the alleyway and wept bitterly.

THE STRANGE TRIAL

Matthew 26:59–75; 27:1–25

Inside the palace hall, the torches had begun to flicker out. The High Priest was getting angry and impatient. No one could truthfully say that Jesus had done anything wrong.

Finally, the priests asked Jesus Himself, "*Are* You the Son of God?"

Jesus answered, "I am. And one day you will see Me seated at My Father's right hand when I come in glory."

The Pharisees and the priests howled. "What more evidence do we need?" They pointed their fingers tauntingly. "This man claims that He is the Son of God. That's *blasphemy*. For that, He must die!"

But the Jews were not allowed to execute anyone without the Roman governor's assent. Therefore Jesus was led away and handed over to Pilate, the governor.

The morning sun rose, red and angry-looking, over Jerusalem. People stood in the streets, staring up at the thin, black clouds that hovered like a frown. Mothers held their children close.

And then the grim news sped through the city. "The priests and Pharisees have arrested Jesus. They are taking Him to Pilate, the Roman governor, to be sentenced."

Many of Jesus' followers were in Jerusalem for the Passover. Mary, His mother, had come with a group of women. Frightened by the news, they ran through the market place where they met John, the youngest apostle.

The temple guards were pushing Jesus through the streets toward Pilate's mansion. Their captive's shoulders sagged with weariness, for Jesus had stood all night through the long trial.

When they reached Pilate's house, the priests and Pharisees complained, "This man claims that He is the Son of God. And His followers want to make Him king of the Jews. But it is illegal for us to put Him to death without your judgment."

Pilate looked at Jesus. "Are you the king of the Jews?" he asked.

"You have spoken rightly," Jesus answered. "But My kingdom is not an earthly kingdom. If it were, My men would be fighting to save Me right now."

Pilate turned to the priests and Pharisees. "This man has not broken any Roman law. So you will have to take Him to your own King Herod."

When Herod saw Jesus standing in his throne room, he was overjoyed. "Miracle-man, if you'll perform a miracle for me, I just might let You go," he offered slyly.

But Jesus refused to perform a miracle. Nor would He answer any of Herod's questions. In anger, Herod sent Him back to Pilate.

By now Pilate was very annoyed with the Jewish priests. "I've already told you that I find no fault in this man. Even Herod found no reason to condemn Him. So now? What do you want me to do with this Jesus?"

"Crucify him! Crucify him!" they shouted.

Pilate called for a bowl of water. Dipping his hands in the bowl, he declared, "I wash my hands of this case. I am not guilty of killing this innocent man. You may do what you like with Him."

With that Pilate turned Jesus over to his garrison of Roman soldiers.

THAT TERRIBLE DAY!
Luke 23:1–47

To the soldiers Jesus was just another criminal to be crucified. So they flogged His bare back with thin leather thongs, hit Him again and again with their fists, and spat in His face. Then they dressed Him in a robe of purple. Cutting branches from a thorn bush, they wove a crown and shoved the sharp spikes down onto His head.

As blood trickled down His face, the soldiers mockingly bowed before Him, "Hail, king of the Jews!"

But through all this abuse, Jesus did not protest or cry out.

Finally, the soldiers led Him into the street outside and laid upon His already bleeding back a rough, wooden cross. He was to drag it through the city streets. As the sun beat down, several times He stumbled and fell under the heavy weight.

It seemed as if all of Jerusalem stood along the streets watching. Jesus' mother was there and so many who loved Him. They could not hold back tears when they saw His sad face and heard the painful scraping of the cross on the cobblestone street. Yet they could only watch helplessly.

Jesus staggered on past the city wall. The soldiers drove Him up a hill called Golgotha—"the skull," where criminals were executed.

Here, they laid the cross on the ground and nailed His hands

Lightning flashed as Jesus died on the Cross

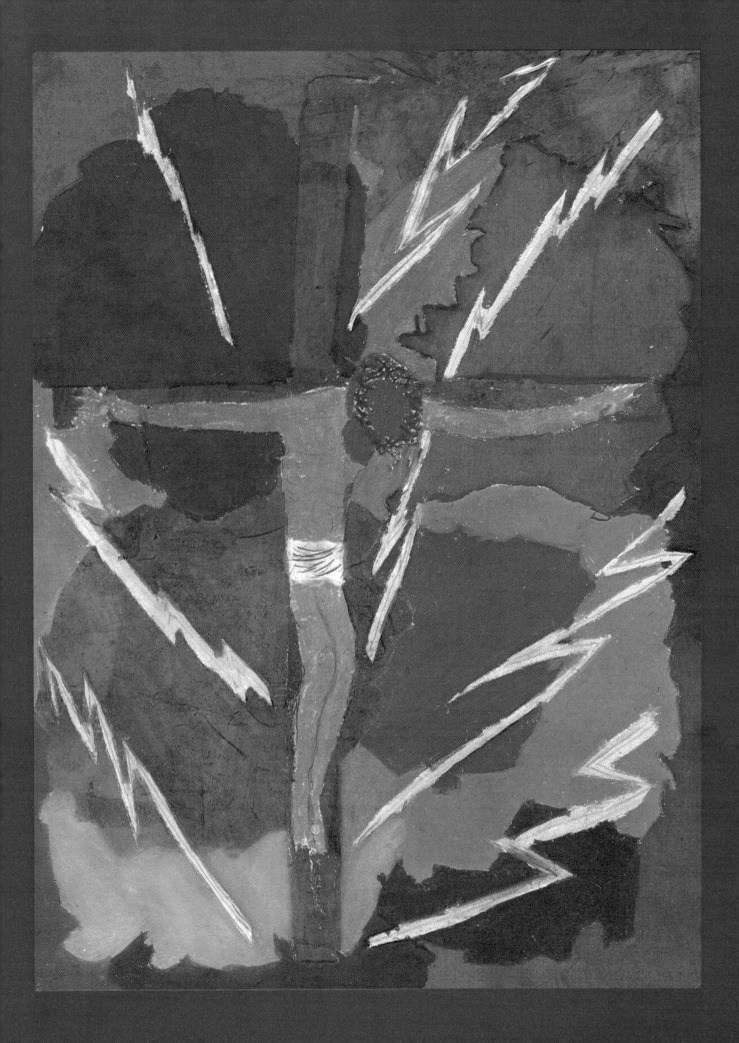

and feet to it. Then they raised the cross up, setting it between two convicted thieves who were also being crucified. High in the air, Jesus hung like a common thief.

Jesus' mother Mary also climbed the hill with a few of the women who had followed Him. John, the apostle, was there too. He held Mary tightly as she cried for her son.

Even through His pain, Jesus was thinking of others. He nodded His head toward John. "This will be your son," He told Mary tenderly.

To John, He said, "She will be your mother now. Take care of her, John."

As the hours went by, the crowd scarcely noticed that the sun was being swallowed by huge, black clouds. By late afternoon, thunder rumbled angrily in the hills.

The soldiers did not notice either; they were too busy gambling for Jesus' clothes.

One of the thieves was still taunting Jesus. "Why don't you rescue us? You are supposed to be such a great miracle worker!"

The other thief silenced him. "Leave Jesus alone. We deserve to die for our crimes. But He is innocent."

Then he made a request of Jesus. "Master, remember me when You enter Your kingdom."

Jesus raised His head and spoke in a painful whisper. "*Today* you will be with Me in Paradise."

Now the wind came gusting through the hills and valleys. The soldiers drew their cloaks tightly about them as rain whipped their faces.

Suddenly, Jesus cried out from His cross, "It is *finished!* Father, into Your hands I entrust My Spirit."

Then His head fell forward.

He was dead.

Thunder roared. An earthquake shook all of Jerusalem. The Roman soldiers ran to and fro as lightning lashed the sky.

In the temple, the veil that covered the Holy of Holies was torn in two from top to bottom. The priests fell on their faces in terror.

At the top of Golgotha, the captain of the Roman soldiers, awestruck, stood under the three crosses. Looking up at Jesus, he said, awe in his voice, "Truly, this Man was the Son of God!"

A strange darkness was over all the land. Jesus' followers came and took Him down from the cross. Mary knelt and cradled His limp body as she wept.

The other women wrapped His broken, bloody body in grave cloths. Then they hurried to lay Him in a tomb, for it was almost night.

Even this was not enough for the priests and Pharisees. They went to Pilate again.

"Jesus' followers may steal His body from the tomb, and then tell everyone He has risen from the dead. If so, things will be much worse than before. Send some of your soldiers to guard His tomb," they pleaded.

But Pilate sent them away angrily. "Send your own guards," he said.

So the temple guards were sent to roll a huge, heavy boulder in front of the tomb. They sealed the opening, and stood guarding it, day and night.

Now the priests and Pharisees clapped one another on the back. "We have seen the last of this Jesus of Nazareth," they boasted.

Women gathered at the tomb

THE EMPTY TOMB

Luke 24:1–9; John 20:1–18

It was early morning, three days after Jesus had been crucified. Just at sunup, a group of women who had followed Jesus were on their way to His tomb.

In the low, green valleys, mist trailed like a soft gauze scarf. In the trees, birds were singing joyfully. The fields and hills seemed alive with some bright hope.

But the women did not notice. They walked slowly, sadly, their heads bowed. The day Jesus had died, they had not had time to bury Him properly, according to custom. Now each one carried spices and perfumes to anoint His lifeless body.

One of the women spoke up. "Who will roll away the heavy stone for us?" she asked.

"The soldiers of the high Priest are still guarding the tomb," another said. "Perhaps they will help us."

They rounded another bend in the path, and saw the tomb up ahead. But something strange had happened.

The temple guards were gone, and the huge boulder had been rolled to one side. Not only that, from the tomb a bright light glowed.

Now the women started running. As they thrust their heads inside the tomb, they were startled to see an angel standing before them. His robe was white as snow and as brilliant as lightning.

"Don't be afraid," he said. "I know you are looking for Jesus of Nazareth. He is not here. He has risen from the dead, just as He promised you."

Now, almost too excited to breathe, the women stared at the empty tomb. The grave cloths were lying in the floor. But Jesus was nowhere to be seen.

The angel urged them, "Go quickly and tell His disciples!"

So the women drew up their skirts and ran from the tomb, their faces glowing with the wonderful news to tell Peter and John and the others.

An angel stood guard

What the women did not know was that one of their group had already been there before them. That same morning, while it was still dark, Mary Magdalene, one of Jesus' special friends, had come to the tomb. She too had found the stone rolled away and the tomb empty.

Then did that mean, she had wondered, that someone had stolen her beloved Master's body? Trying to think this through, Mary had sat weeping outside the tomb.

All at once she had looked up to see a man step out of the shadowy trees. Through her blinding tears, Mary had thought Him the gardener.

"Woman," the Man had said, "why are you crying?"

"My Master's body has been stolen," she had sobbed. "Did You take Him away?"

The Man had come closer and had spoken gently. "Mary," was all He had said.

She had looked up, her eyes growing wide. Only one voice in the world spoke like that! It was Jesus Himself standing before her, smiling.

"Master!" She had flung herself at His feet.

"Yes, it is I—alive, as I told you I would be. Hurry, Mary. Go tell My brothers that you have seen Me. Soon I will be taken up to God, to My Father and to your Father."

So Mary had run back to Jerusalem. There she had found the disciples still in hiding for fear of the Jews. Judas was no longer with them, for in his disgust at what he had done, he had hanged himself.

When Mary reached the house where they were hiding, the disciples were arguing with the other women. "There's no way Jesus can be alive. What kind of silly tales are you trying to put over on us?"

Now a radiant Mary reported, "But it's *true!* I have seen Jesus myself with my own eyes. He *is* alive!"

Peter and John then ran to see for themselves. They found the grave cloths just as the women had said. But they did not yet see Jesus Himself.

JESUS RETURNS

John 20:19–21; Luke 24:33–45; John 21:1–19

That evening the disciples again met secretly. They even drew an iron bolt across the door and latched the shutters so no light could shine from the windows.

Some of the disciples still did not believe the glad tidings Mary and the other women had brought them. "These women have to be mistaken. We *know* Jesus is dead. Probably they saw a ghost."

At that moment a familiar voice spoke from behind them. "Greetings! Peace be with you."

They peered into the shadow by the door. There stood Jesus. And the iron bar was still drawn.

He walked into their midst and sat down by the fire.

"Yes, I am really your Master. See, touch Me." He smiled. "A ghost doesn't have flesh and blood." He turned the palms of His hands outward, showing the wounds where the nails had pierced Him.

At last the disciples believed. They hugged each other and laughed. Then they hugged each other all over again. Their own Master, their beloved Lord, was with them once more.

Jesus sat with them far into the night, eating fish and honeycomb.

"It was necessary for Me to suffer for the sins of the whole world," He explained to them. "There was no other way to make right the sin of the first man, Adam, except through Me."

He told them, "I am going to leave you with a special mission. Soon you must go and tell everyone the truth: tell them that I was dead, but now I am alive forevermore."

But then, all at once, Jesus was no longer there: He had disappeared.

And the bolt was still in place across the closed door.

The disciples did not rush out to tell everyone that they had seen Jesus. Perhaps they were afraid people would laugh and not believe them. So for a time, they went back to their own villages.

One morning Peter and John and some of the other disciples were fishing on the Sea of Galilee. The sun was rising as they lowered their nets into the green, foaming water. Then they sat down to wait in the gently rocking boat.

After a long time they drew in their nets. Empty. . . They had caught no fish at all. Only dripping seaweed clung to the ropes.

They were about to give up when a Stranger called out from the distant shore. "Lower your net on the other side of the boat," He shouted.

The disciples looked at one another. The voice sounded familiar. Could it be? . . . Once before Jesus had called to them from the same shore.

So, obediently, they lowered their net again. At once hundreds of splashing fish silvered the water. The net was filled to the breaking point.

John looked at the Man on the shore. Excitedly, he turned to Peter. "Peter, it's the *Lord!*"

Jesus was waiting for them on the sandy beach. He sat broiling fish over a cheerful fire.

After He had fed them a hearty breakfast, He turned to Peter, looking directly at him. "Do you love Me, Peter?" Jesus asked.

"Lord, You *know* that I love You—"

"Then feed My sheep."

Peter was puzzled when Jesus asked the same question two more times.

Then, suddenly, he understood. This was Jesus' way of telling him, "I forgive you, Peter, for denying Me three times. But now, I have work for you to do: you are to spend the rest of your life telling others about My forgiveness and My love for them too."

Then Jesus told the whole group, "Go back to Jerusalem. Gather My followers on the Mount of Olives. I will meet you there."

And saying that, He disappeared.

THE GIFT OF NEW POWER

Acts 1:1–14; 2:1–41

Not long afterwards, the disciples stood on the Mount of Olives. Five hundred of Jesus' other followers were there too.

As they waited quietly, Jesus appeared among them. Everyone fell silent. Even the birds and crickets were hushed.

He told them, "Very soon, the Holy Spirit will fall upon you, bringing power from on high. Wait in Jerusalem until I send Him to you. *After* you have received the power of the Spirit, *then* you are to go and tell My story to the farthest ends of the earth."

Even as Jesus was speaking, the sky above Him began to open like a great door. A rushing wind swept over the mountain, and Jesus began to rise slowly through the air.

"Remember," He called to them, "I will be with you always, even until the end of the world." And He disappeared into the clouds.

As all of them stood staring into the sky, two angels appeared.

"Men of Galilee," they said, "why do you stand there looking up into the sky? You have seen Jesus taken from you into Heaven. One day men will see Him return to earth in the same way, with great glory."

Listening to these words, the disciples were filled with joy. As Jesus told them to do, they went back to Jerusalem to await there His promise: "*You will receive power when the Holy Spirit comes upon you. . . .*"

The disciples stood on the Mount of Olives   193

None of them quite understood what to expect. But while they were waiting, about one hundred and twenty of Jesus' followers gathered in one large upper room. Jesus' mother Mary was there too along with some friends and relatives from Nazareth.

It was on the day of Pentecost that Jesus chose to send the gift of the Holy Spirit to them. This was an important Jewish holiday when people from many countries gathered in Jerusalem.

Suddenly the group in the upper room heard a mighty noise: it was as if a strong, driving wind was blowing through all the doors and windows of the house.

And immediately, little flames of fire appeared and rested on the head of each of them.

But the most amazing thing is that the disciples began to speak and to understand languages which they had not known a minute earlier.

This caused a great stir. All who heard were saying, "But these men are all Galileans! How is it that they're now speaking the languages of the Parthians, the Medes, the Cretans, the Romans, the Arabs, and others?

It was the disciple Peter who answered. . .

"Men and brethren, this is the work of the Holy Spirit whose coming Jesus promised us. We are also seeing today the word of the prophet accomplished:

'This will happen in the last days: I will pour out upon everyone a portion of my spirit; and your sons and daughters shall prophesy; your young men shall see visions, and your old men shall dream dreams.'

"This One who was crucified," Peter went on, "was the Son of God. He has been raised from the dead and is alive forevermore. He came to earth to forgive us sinners by bearing our sins in His own body. We are accepted back by God the minute we believe Jesus and give our lives to Him."

"You shall receive power," Jesus told them

On that one day in Jerusalem, three thousand people became disciples of Jesus Christ.

So the truth about Jesus spread: the truth that He was the One sent by God to restore the Garden of Eden to all men who wanted it. Only Eden's name was changed to ''the kingdom of God on earth.'' Jesus' followers travelled like shining lights over the mountains and seas and deserts, to all the cities and lonely places of the world to spread the glad tidings of Jesus' victory over Snake.

The Holy Spirit had given Jesus' disciples not only peace and great joy, but a wonderful love so that they shared everything they had with others.

He also gave the new disciples the ability to heal the sick, as Jesus had done, and to perform many miracles.

Best of all, as they let the Spirit speak through them, men and women really understood the Good News, not just with their minds, but in their hearts.

Jesus is alive. He loves you. Tell Him that you want Him to be your Lord. Then you too can have the joy of His presence, not only with you every day in your work and in your play, but His own Spirit living inside you.

Jesus said, "Tell my story to all the people"